Coaching Beyond Wo

In *Coaching Beyond Words: Using Art to Deepen and Enrich Our Conversations*, Anna Sheather presents a practical guide for those seeking to incorporate art in their own coaching practice. Complete with case studies and art created by clients, Anna explores how coaching with art connects clients to a deeper level of personal awareness and understanding, which in turn leads to meaningful shifts in personal growth, development and fulfilment.

Anna offers the coach an exciting and transformative way to work with their clients by bridging the gap between art and coaching. She covers how to introduce creative approaches, how to support creativity and how to work with the art produced, opening enriching coaching conversations with clients. The author combines her personal experiences with research that underpins her practice, exploring the benefits of the interdisciplinary nature of art therapy and neuroscience by looking at the field of hemispherical lateralisation to help understand why coaching with art works so effectively. The book also provides a comprehensive guide of how to prepare an art coaching session, including contracting, an overview of types of exercises, key principles and approaches to facilitating the image making process, overcoming barriers with coachees and guidance on managing oneself in the process, including managing boundaries. *Coaching Beyond Words* is the first book to provide an in-depth look at the importance and practicality in interweaving coaching and art, and it forms a complete guide to context, theory and practice.

Coaching Beyond Words: Using Art to Deepen and Enrich Our Conversations will appeal to coaches in practice as well as any art therapist seeking to expand their practice into coaching. Additionally, it would be of interest to creative professionals looking to incorporate coaching theory.

Anna Sheather is an executive coach and coach supervisor based in the UK. She has been running her coaching practice, Élan Coaching Ltd, for over a decade. She incorporates her passion for art, painting and creativity into her professional and personal life.

"*Coaching Beyond Words* is an excellent introduction to using art in coaching. The book focuses on the next generation of coaching that moves beyond the normal question and reflection coaching methodology. It is a delightful mix of theory – from art therapy and neuroscience – and practical insights – from contracting to the art materials needed. I really like the case studies showing the art that clients drew. It brings the concept to life. The book introduces a very practical framework to prepare and enable coaches to get started coaching beyond words."

– **Gil Schwenk, Coaching Supervisor**

"In her primer to any coach wanting to weave the use of art into their coaching to enhance their practice, and offer clients the opportunity to further their coaching, as the title says, literally beyond words, Anna has generously shared her approach to art in coaching with a passion for two things she believes in: the transformational power of art combined with that of coaching. Starting off with what she wants to share, how working with art deepens and enriches coaching conversations, Anna draws parallels to the power of art therapy but makes clear distinctions from art therapy and acknowledges the boundaries between them. Her reassurance to the coach to be confident in their own 'art story' but not needing to be an artist is woven throughout Anna's approach. Her exploration of how art is perceived in the coaching world and the questions she asks coaches to reflect on for themselves draws the reader in to experience the book on an interactive level. Her use of case studies and their testimonials to bring examples of art in coaching to life is a wonderful balance to the more theoretical aspects of the book.

Coaching Beyond Words is an engaging, interactive, well organized and practical book for any coach wanting to apply Anna's technique of art in coaching with confidence to their own coaching practice."

– **Cyndy Walker, MA; HCPC Registered art therapist; BAAT full member**

Coaching Beyond Words

Using Art to Deepen and Enrich
Our Conversations

Anna Sheather

Routledge
Taylor & Francis Group
LONDON AND NEW YORK

First published 2019
by Routledge
2 Park Square, Milton Park, Abingdon, Oxon OX14 4RN

and by Routledge
52 Vanderbilt Avenue, New York, NY 10017

Routledge is an imprint of the Taylor & Francis Group, an informa business

© 2019 Anna Sheather

The right of Anna Sheather to be identified as author of this work has been asserted by her in accordance with sections 77 and 78 of the Copyright, Designs and Patents Act 1988.

All rights reserved. No part of this book may be reprinted or reproduced or utilised in any form or by any electronic, mechanical, or other means, now known or hereafter invented, including photocopying and recording, or in any information storage or retrieval system, without permission in writing from the publishers.

Trademark notice: Product or corporate names may be trademarks or registered trademarks, and are used only for identification and explanation without intent to infringe.

British Library Cataloguing-in-Publication Data
A catalogue record for this book is available from the British Library

Library of Congress Cataloging-in-Publication Data
Names: Sheather, Anna, 1962- author.
Title: Coaching beyond words : using art to deepen and enrich our conversations / Anna Sheather.
Description: Abingdon, Oxon ; New York, NY : Routledge, 2019. | Includes bibliographical references. |
Identifiers: LCCN 2018045747 (print) | LCCN 2018047768 (ebook) | ISBN 9781351166003 (Master eBook) | ISBN 9781351165990 (Adobe Reader) | ISBN 9781351165983 (ePub) | ISBN 9781351165976 (Mobipocket) | ISBN 9780815348733 (hardback) | ISBN 9780815348740 (pbk.)
Subjects: LCSH: Art therapy. | Personal coaching. | Art and psychology.
Classification: LCC RC489.A7 (ebook) | LCC RC489.A7 S54 2019 (print) | DDC 616.89/1656—dc23
LC record available at https://lccn.loc.gov/2018045747

ISBN: 978-0-8153-4873-3 (hbk)
ISBN: 978-0-8153-4874-0 (pbk)
ISBN: 978-1-351-16600-3 (ebk)

Typeset in Times New Roman
by Swales & Willis Ltd, Exeter, Devon, UK

Contents

List of Figures vii
List of Plates viii
Acknowledgements ix

1 **Introduction to coaching with art** 1

   My research 3
   Talking and working with other coaches 4
   About the book 6

2 **Art and communication** 8

3 **Art therapy and coaching** 12

   The benefits 13
   The approach 14
   What happens? 15

4 **Art and the brain hemispheres** 18

   Research into the functions of the brain
      hemispheres 19
   Hemisphere function and coaching with art 23
   Right-hemisphere time-free mode 37
   Quietening the left hemisphere 38
   Bringing the hemispheres together 39

5 **Art and coaching** 42

   Next-generation coaching 43
   Coaching in today's world 43

Benefits of using an art-based approach 44
The applications of coaching with art 46
Barriers to using art in coaching 51
Limitations to coaching with art 55

6   The principles of coaching with art — 57

The core principles 58
The coach 62
The client 63
Supervision 63

7   Coaching with art in practice — 64

I Contracting for coaching with art 65
II Preparing for coaching with art 68
III The first session 71
IV Overcoming clients' potential barriers 71
V Which exercise? 72
VI Facilitating the process for our clients 78
VII Managing ourselves in this process 87
VIII Boundaries and ethics 89
IX The final session and closing out 90

8   Materials — 92

Supports 93
Drawing mediums 94
Painting and water-based mediums 95
Other mediums 96
Accessories 97
Storing your materials 97
Where to buy 97

9   Getting started — 99

Building confidence in your own creativity 99
Developing your confidence in coaching with art 102
Being prepared 104

References and further resources — 108
Index — 110

Figures

1.1	An example of a client's art created in a coaching session	2
4.1	The left- and right-hemisphere crossover; illustration by the author	22
4.2	Drawn by the author, based on a drawing by E.G. Boring (1930), taken from a German postcard from 1888	25
4.3	Spiral staircase; illustration by the author	26
7.1	Coaching-with-art framework	65
7.2	James' first image from his second coaching session	81
7.3	James' new image, created from cutting up and adding to his first image	82
7.4	The Karpman Drama Triangle	88

Plates

Colour Image 1   Sam's image of her and the organisation, showing the whole issue and the complexity within it
Colour Image 2   Sam's transformational image of a curl
Colour Image 3   Amelia's desert island; a representation of her new relationship
Colour Image 4   Amelia's aha! moment
Colour Image 5   Keira's breakthrough image 'flow'
Colour Image 6   Keira's breakthrough image 'inner voice'
Colour Image 7   James' final images: 'where I was', 'where I am now' and 'where I want to be'
Colour Image 8   Jaye's first image from her first coaching session
Colour Image 9   Jaye's final image showing her shift out of 'stuckness'
Colour Image 10   James' image from a guided exercise
Colour Image 11   Sam's image from a guided metaphor-based exercise
Colour Image 12   Amelia's initial play image, added to through exploration and coaching in her first session
Colour Image 13   James' final image
Colour Image 14   Sam's final image

Acknowledgements

The writing of this book has come about through the support and encouragement, as well as the contribution, from coaching colleagues, friends and family. When Susannah Frearson at Routledge gave me the opportunity to do this, it was only because those colleagues who came on early pilot workshops listened to my ideas and were so encouraging that I had the confidence to say yes. Then there are my five clients who have given me permission to share their coaching experiences in this book as case studies. You know who you are – and thank you. This book would not have worked without your contributions. I would also like to say a big thank you to Gil Schwenk, Jerry Gilpin and Anne Butler, who made time to read and comment on the book as I drafted it. Gil, who is also my supervisor, was the catalyst for starting off my exploration into art in coaching, as it was in one our sessions that I had my aha! moment that led to all of this. I would also like to say thank you to Cyndy Walker, who is the art therapist I engage as a coach and who has given me the space to work out what I want to do and enabled me to experience working this way as a client.

Thank you to all the coaches and clients that I have met along the way who I have had the privilege to work with, not only as I developed my art-based practice, but also over the many years of learning and growing as a coach.

Thank you also to John Morley (www.johnmorleyphotography.co.uk) who photographed the images in the book and did it all just before going on holiday so I could meet my deadline. The images tell as much of the story as the words.

Last, I want to say a big thank you to friends and family who have listened to me as I have struggled, encouraged me to keep going and distracted me when I got stuck.

Chapter 1
Introduction to coaching with art

> *'I have found that coaching beyond words through using art is an amazing and fast way to access that deeper, embodied level of self-awareness that often creates those shifts. Even if shifts don't occur, there always seems to be a greater sense of personal meaning and understanding that unlocks something for that person.'*
> Anna Sheather

In this book I want to share with you how working with art deepens and enriches our coaching conversations, moving our clients beyond words to a much deeper level of awareness, understanding and personal meaning that can, and often does, create transformational shifts.

I am an executive coach who paints, and through my experiences of working with art in coaching I firmly believe art has an important role in our practice. When I talk about art, I am not talking about creating great masterpieces; I am talking about any image a client creates that has personal meaning to them. This image could be a drawing, a sculpture, a painting, a collage or a mixture. It is about self-expression – externalising, through line, colour, texture and form an image of their interior selves. It is about working intuitively, going with what feels right in the moment, without censorship and judgement.

A client does not need to be able to draw or to consider themselves to be creative to work in this way; they just have to be open to the experience and willing to push themselves a little out of their comfort zone.

Although I am a self-taught artist, there is also no requirement for a coach to be an artist to use this approach. What you do need is to feel confident working in this way and to be really familiar with the materials you are offering your client to work with. It means being comfortable with creativity and being open to your own creative self. In Chapter 5, I look at this in more detail and invite you to explore your own art story. I also talk more about getting started and building confidence in your practice in Chapter 9.

My approach to coaching with art was in one way just happened upon, but has also been the product of quite a lot of research, experience and practice – and I am still learning.

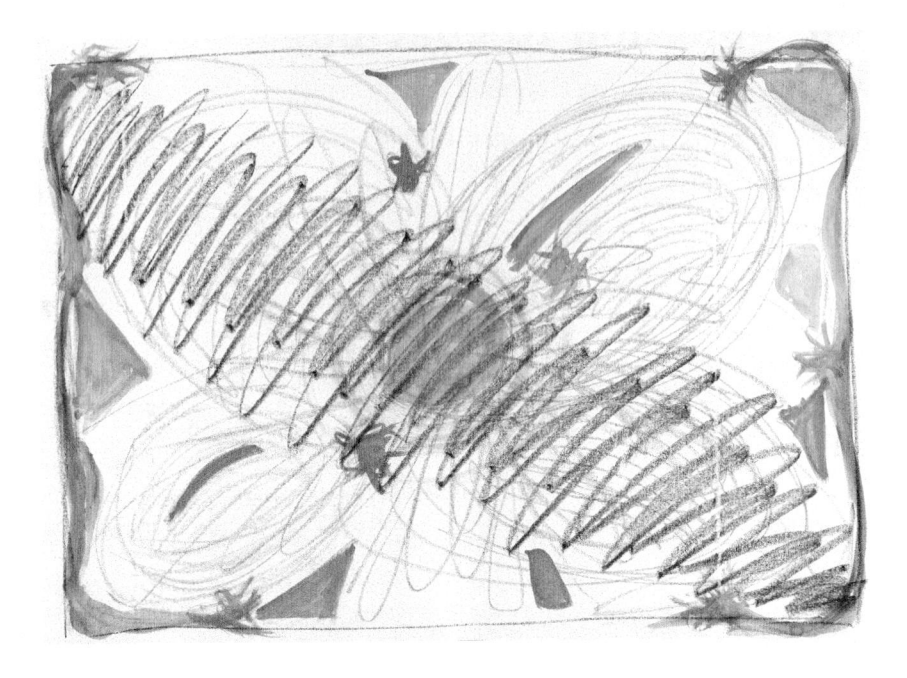

Figure 1.1 An example of a client's art created in a coaching session

When I say it was just happened upon, I mean it was a moment that came from a conversation with my supervisor. One January a couple of years ago, I came to a supervision session feeling jaded with my coaching. I had been running my executive coaching practice for many years and had noticed that my enthusiasm was waning. One of the main reasons I had left mainstream employment to become self-employed was to enable me to make time for my creative side. Over those years my creative life had grown and I was holding this very separate from me as a coach, even though I knew that I coach at my best when I coach from who I am. I was stuck.

In that session, my supervisor said, 'the great thing about what we do is we can put our energy where we want to'. It was my aha! moment, and the rest, as they say, is history. I had already started to explore the possibility of using art in my coaching and had been drawn to art therapy, wondering if I needed to retrain. But I knew my passion was with coaching.

In addition to exploring art therapy, I had been, and still am, intrigued by archaeological discoveries that show how human beings have been using art to communicate for many, many thousands of years. I was also fascinated by the right-hemisphere/left-hemisphere ways of seeing the world and, linked to that, I had just started exploring mindfulness and creativity. I was already building the foundations for my practice. This then formed the starting point for my more formal research. How could I integrate art into my coaching practice, including my executive coaching?

My research

My research has taken me down four main avenues, and to help put my approach into context I have summarised these below. Each of these avenues has been further expanded in the chapters that follow.

1   **Art and communication.** Through my interest in ancient archaeology, I learnt that art is a form of communication that pre-dates written and verbal language and we human beings have used it for tens of thousands of years to communicate our place in the world, our ideas, our feelings and our perceptions. Psychology has also found that using image making allows people to externalise and understand that which otherwise they find difficult and/or impossible to articulate.
2   **Art therapy and coaching.** Art therapy is a form of psychotherapy that uses art as a powerful means of communication, which has shown me the potential that working with art in coaching can have. It has also provided me with the initial insights into how art can be used in coaching and the benefits it can bring. I have been particularly drawn to Liesl Stevenson's person-centred approach to art therapy, which has many similarities to coaching. I also engaged an art therapist to work on my own personal development and to experience it from a client's perspective. This has been invaluable, enabling me to experience the process, how it feels and what happens.
3   **Art and the hemispheres of the brain.** Following my curiosity with right-hemisphere/left-hemisphere functions, I wanted to see what evidence there was in neuroscience that could explain why an art-based approach is so effective. Art is often seen as 'fluffy' and grounding it more scientifically could start to change this perception. I was helped enormously by Ian McGilchrist's book *The Master and His Emissary*. Although McGilchrist's book is about the social, political and philosophical implications of the lateralisation of the brain (the division of the brain into the right and left hemispheres), he starts by looking at the research and discussion around the different functions of the hemispheres. This research started to give me some evidence and clues as to how the right hemisphere could be playing an important role in this type of coaching. Through this work I have also come to understand the importance of both hemispheres of the brain, and how working with art in coaching can bring the hemispheres together. One of the key areas was finding ways to enable the right-hemisphere way of perceiving the world to be communicated. This led me to exploring mindfulness as a means of helping people connect at a deeper level. Through research and attending an eight-week mindfulness course, I learnt how to create a space in a coaching session for a client's image to emerge. I also found that it doesn't work for everyone and that other approaches can be very effective in the right circumstances.
4   **Art and coaching.** The research above was only a starting point and it has been learning through practice and experience that has enabled me to develop my approach. This has not only included coaching with art, but also running workshops and CPD events for other coaches who are interested in integrating

art into their own practice. This experience has been invaluable for not only hearing what coaches think about this approach, but also for understanding what stops coaches from working this way. Here, I have been fascinated by how our own perceptions of art and artists, and our confidence in our own creativity, limit what we do. I have been fascinated by how these perceptions arise from our own 'art stories'. To expand my learning and start some research into how this approach works, I set up coaching case studies where art was the central approach. This also enabled me to test out art-based coaching's relevance to executive and business coaching as people's perceptions were starting to box this into an approach for creative or life issues. To do this, I worked with five clients and the case studies include executive, business and life issues as well as creativity issues. This work has deepened my understanding of this approach, reinforced the benefits and outcomes, demonstrated clearly how coaches need to hold an art-based coaching space and shown me that this approach has relevance for all sorts of coaching. I would like to say a big thank you to my clients for allowing me to share their stories in this book, although to maintain confidentiality and respect privacy their names and some of the context has been changed.

Throughout my research and practice, I have been very aware of the boundaries to using art in coaching. This approach has the ability to take clients to hidden places that they may not have expected and either may not be ready for or may not want to go to. It also means that this approach may inadvertently take coaches to spaces they are not skilled to coach in, or are not qualified to coach in. To manage these boundaries, coaches need to use this approach with clear and positive intent, ensuring they are coaching within the contract and coaching guidelines and ethics. I expand on this further in Chapter 6, where I pull together the core principles of coaching with art.

Talking and working with other coaches

Throughout my learning and practice I have been able to talk with coaches from different backgrounds – internal and independent, new and experienced – and I have been really surprised at how many coaches are interested in this area. I have met many coaches who want to develop a creative side to their practice and others who are already using art in their work and want to build on it. I have talked to coaches who take their clients to art galleries, using the art as a starting point for a conversation, some who use picture cards and others who work with collage, dance, music or poetry.

I have also had animated conversations about how transformational coaches have found a session has gone when working with art. However, I also hear coaches limit this approach, stating that they couldn't work this way in, for example, a client's office as they may be seen as 'playing', with the client perhaps wondering why they are paying them to coach. I have heard statements such as 'you can't bring this into the boardroom' or 'my clients wouldn't work this way'.

The word 'art' seems to polarise people and cause them to judge themselves. People tend to see art as either something rarefied and elitist, with comments such as 'I can't draw' or 'I am not at all creative' or 'I am not an artist!', or it is seen as something children do – playing and messing around – and isn't something that 'I' as an adult would do. It seems art is either something of very high value and 'I' am excluded, or it is of very low value and not something 'I' would do. Interestingly, we are very quick to box it; we are almost fearful of it and are often very dismissive of it. The exception to this is if I am working with coaches who are creative. However, even these coaches can still worry about the perception others have of them if they use art in a coaching session.

> Take a moment and pause...
> What are your thoughts about art?
> How might they be shaping your perception of this book? Or about your ability to use art in coaching?
> Note them down. Be open and honest with yourself. No one else is going to see them.
> I now invite you to hold them with curiosity and without judgement as you continue to read the book.

Next-generation coaching

Whilst talking with coaches, they often start referring to this approach as next-generation or second-generation coaching. It feels as though coaches are looking for something 'else' in their coaching practice, something that is deeper, more intuitive and transformational – perhaps wanting to move beyond models and processes.

This may be because one of the most valued outcomes in coaching is when clients have that transformational shift that unlocks change. It is a bit like magic and we don't always know why or how it happens. I have found that coaching beyond words through using art is an amazing and fast way to access that deeper, embodied level of self-awareness that often creates those shifts. Even if shifts don't occur, there always seems to be a greater sense of personal meaning and understanding that unlocks something for that person.

Also, I believe that people are increasingly coming to coaching for that shift, that deeper level of awareness that creates lasting personal change, whether it is in their professional or personal lives. Using art can do this powerfully and quietly, as long as the person being coached is open to the process.

I also think we are looking for faster ways of working. There seem to be two main drivers for this. First, we work in a world where there is instant gratification, which inevitably raises expectations around coaching. Second, organisational clients often limit the spend on external coaching and the number of sessions available to employees, whilst at the same time there is an expectation that much will be achieved! One of the benefits I have found using art is that it can unlock core issues very quickly and often much faster than pure verbal coaching. As a result, I have been able to start working with my clients at a deeper and more transformational level earlier in the programme.

Another great benefit is that coaching programmes can be measured more consciously and tangibly. This is because the images created are 'keepable' and memorable, allowing you to look back over the coaching programme and clearly see the coaching outcomes and benefits from the sessions. I know from experience that when I do this with clients who have not used art, it can be harder to gauge the extent of the progress as people often forget what it was like for them at the beginning and find it difficult to articulate what has changed for them. Words can also be forgotten, misremembered or exchanged for other words that may mean something slightly different.

About the book

As I mentioned at the beginning, through my own learning and practice of coaching with art I firmly believe this approach has an important role in our practice. I am continually learning, and I hope that by sharing my discoveries and practice with you it gives you the confidence to start to explore the possibility of integrating art into your own practice.

The book essentially falls into two parts. The first part is based on my research and learning that forms the foundations of this approach. Chapter 2 looks at art and communication, expanding into an overview of art therapy and how it crosses over in to coaching (Chapter 3). In Chapter 4 I look at the neuroscience that is starting to shed light on why these approaches work so effectively and, in particular, the research into the functions of the right and left hemispheres of the brain. I finish part one with Chapter 5, where I talk about the relevance and practice of art in coaching today, including the benefits to clients and coaches, and its applications.

The second part of the book is the 'how-to' part. In Chapter 6, I bring together the core principles on which my practice is based, followed by a detailed look at how I coach with art (Chapter 7). This includes:

- how to introduce and work with art in coaching following a five-step approach with a focus on being client-centred; the five steps are (1) imaging, (2) creating, (3) connecting, (4) coaching and (5) continuing discoveries; examples from the case studies are included as well as tips and hints from my own practice
- the boundaries of coaching with art and how to keep a coaching focus
- how to manage ourselves in this process
- unlocking barriers to this approach

In Chapter 8, I explore the materials you can include in your practice, looking at their properties and how you can use them. This is then followed, in Chapter 9, by some guidance on getting started, including hints and tips to build your confidence with coaching with art, as well as putting together a starter pack of materials.

To get the best from this book I encourage you to be open-minded, to be willing to try things out and to turn off your inner judgement of your own creativity. Hold your thoughts, perceptions and judgements with curiosity and explore with me the ways in which art can help you coach beyond words.

References

Malik, Kenan (2013). 'Divided Brain, Divided World?' *Pandaemonium* blog, 21 February. Retrieved from https://kenanmalik.wordpress.com/2013/02/21/divided-brain-divided-world.

McGilchrist, Iain (2012). *The Master and His Emissary: The Divided Brain and the Making of the Western World*. Princeton, NJ: Yale University Press.

Chapter 2

Art and communication

> '...we all have the same remarkable, complex brain that enables us to imagine and communicate ideas beyond words in images and through music.'
> Neil MacGregor, Director's Foreword in Jill Cook's
> Ice-age Art: Arrival of the Modern Mind

Art is a powerful means of communicating and the old adage 'a picture paints a thousand words' is very true. When we look at visual images, whether they are painted, drawn, sculpted or photographed, we connect with them, even if that connection is unconscious and subliminal. A lot of advertising works in this way. Our connection is an emotional one that takes us to our memories and links us to places, people and experiences, bringing them to the present moment.

Art can draw us in, and we start to look deeper, interpreting what we see. We may make comments about what art is about, how good it is, whether we like it or not. We may start to find our own meanings, perspectives and understanding in the image. Art communicates to us.

People create art as a means of expressing themselves and to communicate their perspectives and place in the world; human beings have been doing this for many thousands of years. We are perhaps most familiar with cave paintings, where we see images drawn and painted in earth colours of bison, horses and people. However, archaeologists have also discovered beautiful artefacts dating from at least 40,000 years ago. These include sculptures, engravings, exquisitely drawn images on weapons and tools and jewellery. There are artefacts of the female form as well as images of animals and people hunting. All of these images communicate our ancient ancestors' place in their world, as well as how they felt and thought about their world.

In 2013, The British Museum put on an exhibition of prehistoric art called 'Ice-age Art: Arrival of the Modern Mind', 'illustrating the fundamental desire to communicate and make art as a way of understanding ourselves and our place in the world' (Cook, 2013). Alongside these artefacts, modern art works were displayed, including sculptures and paintings by Pablo Picasso, Lucien Freud, Henri Matisse and Henry Moore. When seeing the ancient and modern side by side, one can't help but see a connection across those many thousands of years. For example, when looking at the 'Woman from Willendorf' sculpture, which is 20,000–30,000 years old, and comparing it to the paintings of women by Freud, Matisse and Picasso, the similarities of form and shape are evident. These similarities connect us to the people who made these artefacts and also lead us to interpret what they may mean. Of course, we don't actually know their true purpose and meaning, but we can make informed judgements not only based on archaeological evidence but also on our own responses to them.

Our use of written language, by comparison, is quite new. The first known written language is Sumerian, which is thought to have emerged around 3300–3000 BC. It is a logographic language, based on images, rather than phonetics. The most well known visual language is probably that of the Egyptian hieroglyphs and today we still see visual language in, for example, Chinese writing.

The phonetic alphabet is even younger, with the earliest phonetic language thought to have arrived around 1200 BC. The rise of phonetic languages and the ability to write things down has been an enormous breakthrough for the development of the human race. It may also be why the left hemisphere has become more dominant than the right hemisphere, as we have been able to expand our ability to categorise and analyse the world around us and develop reasoning and logical exploration across many different areas. This will be explored in Chapter 4, looking at art and the brain hemispheres.

Art still has a very big place in our culture, but it isn't seen as a mainstream way for us to communicate with each other; we don't use it as part of our everyday communication. It is a nice-to-have, and not everyone deems art important or necessary. Or, at least we may think it isn't. Our culture is actually permeated by visual art. If we think about Instagram and Pinterest, and the fact that any social media post only really attracts attention if it has a visual image with it, this suggests we are regularly using art in our communications. We may not see it as art, but the images we post reflect what we want to say to people about what we are experiencing.

We may not see art as a mainstream way of communicating, but art has become a powerful means of communication in the helping professions. To begin with, visual imagery created by patients was interpreted by doctors and seen as a diagnostic tool. Then in the nineteenth century the idea started to emerge that using visual imagery and art could help patients communicate in a way that aided healing and achieved resolution.

This idea started when psychiatry began to focus on the connections between imagery, human emotions and the unconscious. At this time, Sigmund Freud (1856–1939) developed his theories around dreams and the unconscious, making the link between psyche and visual expression. Freud also thought his patients' difficulties in describing their dreams might be alleviated if they could draw them, although he continued to use a talking approach. It was also Freud who realised that art is closer to the unconscious because our visual perceptions predated our capacity for verbal expression.

Carl Jung (1875–1961), working at the same time, saw that by representing a mood or problem as an image, through dreams or art, individuals could begin to understand it more clearly and deeply, and to experience the emotions contained within it. He also drew himself as a means of exploring his own emotions between 1914 and 1930 (Jung, 2009).

This was followed by the emergence of art therapy in the 1940s, with Adrian Hill in the UK and Margaret Naumburg in the USA being cited as the first therapists to actually ask their clients to draw their dreams and images, rather than just talk about them. Adrian Hill recognised the potential of art as therapy when working with soldiers recovering from tuberculosis during World War I, and modern art therapy is founded on the basic principle that art can heal. Hill first coined the phrase 'art therapy' in 1942. Margaret Naumburg was an American psychologist who used art as the primary approach in her work with adults and children. She used scribble drawing, calling her approach 'dynamically orientated art therapy'.

Art therapy is now a fully recognised psychotherapy, where art is a means of self-expression and a means of communicating, connecting and understanding capable of leading to powerful healing. Art therapists have found that using the language of the visual arts (colours, shapes, lines and images) is a safe way for people to externalise and explore trauma, complex issues and feelings, helping them to make sense of and resolve those complexities in a way that pure talking therapies cannot. We may be most familiar with this approach being used with children to help them communicate. It is also widely used with war veterans and most recently with cancer patients.

Art therapy has moved on from the simple experience of art making as a healing process to a much wider profession, bringing therapeutic benefits that lead to emotional growth as well as promoting both mental and physical wellbeing. The growth of art therapy and the experiential evidence of therapists and their clients demonstrates that using art as a mode of expression and communication has wide-ranging and significant benefits.

Coaching is also a helping profession. Coaches work alongside clients who want to achieve success, attain certain goals, make positive life changes or just want to develop and grow to be the best they can be at that time. To achieve their goals our clients often have to uncover and explore what is holding them back, such as their limiting beliefs. These can be hidden or suppressed, and they may have to face their emotional barriers and make shifts in perspectives to allow for the change they are seeking. When exploring these areas clients may find it difficult to express themselves, there may be complex issues at play and paradoxes to explore. They may get stuck in thought loops or be unable make the breakthroughs they want and need, remaining in unhelpful thinking and behaviour patterns.

These scenarios are not dissimilar to those that art therapists' experience, and it is why I believe that art is a powerful form of communication that can be used in coaching to make significant and lasting differences.

Neuroscience is also starting to give us insights into how and why using art to communicate can be so powerful. In particular, new findings about the different functions of the two hemispheres of the brain and how they perceive the world differently suggests that working in a way that allows the right hemisphere to communicate more consciously is particularly useful for coaching. It is also known that the hemispheres co-operate but also inhibit each other, with one or the other taking charge if it thinks itself best for a task. Working with art often leads to the left hemisphere relinquishing control, allowing the right to come to the fore. I explore this in more detail in Chapter 4.

****

Communicating through visual imagery is and has been a fundamental way in which human beings have communicated from tens of thousands of years ago to the present day. In coaching, it is a way for us to connect to a deeper part of ourselves that can lead to insights that in turn lead to personal development, growth and fulfilment. In the next chapter, I go on to look at art therapy and how this form of psychotherapy crosses over into coaching and has started to shape my practice of coaching with art.

References

Bush, Morgan (2013). 'Adrian Hill, UK Founder of Art Therapy'. London Art Therapy Centre. Retrieved from https://arttherapycentre.com/blog/adrian-hill-uk-founder-art-therapy-morgan-bush-intern/.

Cook, Jill (2013). *Ice-age Art: The Arrival of the Modern Mind.* London: The British Museum Press.

Wikipedia (2017). Entry for 'Margaret Naumberg'. Retrieved from https://en.wikipedia.org/wiki/Margaret_Naumburg.

Jung, Carl (2009). *The Red Book: Liber Novus.* Edited by Sonu Shamdasani. New York: Philemon Foundation and W.W. Norton & Co.

Chapter 3

Art therapy and coaching

> *'I would not have had the experience I did with my coach if I hadn't done the drawing.'*
>
> Ann, coach and workshop participant

Coaching as we know it today is a rich and varied developmental intervention ranging from personal through to performance and executive coaching. A lot of coaching has its roots in therapeutic and counselling models with, for example, coaches specialising in CBT, Gestalt or existential-based coaching. Therefore, it makes sense to look to art therapy as a starting point for research into an art-based approach to coaching.

As explained in the previous chapter, art therapy emerged in the 1940s and there are now considered to be two main approaches, which art therapist Cathy A. Malchiodi describes in *The Art Therapy Sourcebook* (2007).

The first is that the art making process in its own right is health-enhancing and a growth producing experience – that just by experiencing the creative process and 'expressing yourself imaginatively, authentically and spontaneously' it will 'lead to personal fulfilment, emotional reparation and transformation'. The second is the idea that art is a means of 'symbolic communication' and that 'the image process and the image created become significant in enhancing verbal exchange between the person and the therapist and in achieving insight. Here, with therapeutic guidance and support, art can facilitate new understandings and insights. It can help resolve conflicts, solve problems and create new perceptions that lead to positive changes, growth and healing' (Malchiodi, 2007, p. 6).

It is this second approach that I believe relates to coaching, as we do very similar things. In coaching we also create a safe space for our clients to explore and reflect on issues and conflicts. We provide an approach that enables them to work things out for themselves, creating new perceptions that ultimately enable our clients to work towards positive outcomes, personal growth and change.

To understand this more fully and to experience it for myself, I engaged an art therapist to work on some personal areas. This helped me to find out from a client's perspective how it worked, how I felt using this approach and what happened.

I found it a very liberating and powerful process and could see very clearly how using art would work, from a client's perspective, in coaching.

This personal experience and my research into art therapy has highlighted three key areas that have been particularly useful as a starting point for developing my art-based practice. These are:

- **the benefits** that art therapy gives the client over and above emotional healing and wellbeing
- **the approach** that art therapists use when managing their sessions and, in particular, Leisl Silverstone's person-centred approach
- **what happens** in an art therapy session and what the client may experience

The benefits

Art therapists have been recording the benefits of using art for self-expression over and above emotional healing and wellbeing for many years, and it is just starting to be supported by structured research. These benefits are captured in much of the writing and books around art therapy, including the work of the British Association of Art Therapists.

From this experiential evidence we can start to see the potential benefits of working this way with coaching clients and I have summarised below those benefits that therapists have identified that I believe correlate to the work we do as coaches and show the possibilities of coaching with art (Malchiodi, 2007; Silverstone, 1997):

- communicating in a way that words cannot; expressing our internal world of thoughts, feelings, hopes and fears, dreams and aspirations
- making sense of and creating personal meaning in a complex and paradoxical situation, as visual imagery can hold multiple complexities and paradoxes simultaneously
- discovering insights, helping people move beyond limits and find their own personal resources
- creating transformational change, realising personal potential and acting as a catalyst for personal change and growth
- knowing themselves from a new perspective and transforming that perspective
- increasing a sense of wellbeing, self-esteem and self-assurance
- encouraging risk taking and experimentation
- tapping into creative problem solving and intuition through exploring new ideas, new ways of expressing themselves and new ways of seeing
- playfulness, joy and creativity that is cathartic, releasing emotions through the physical activity of art making
- reducing stress as the process of art making increases the brain levels of serotonin and engages the relaxation response
- enriching life and achieving self-actualisation through enhancing our abilities, knowing ourselves, reaching our full potential and finding meaning in life

As mentioned above, formal research to prove anecdotal evidence from therapists and their patients is just starting, and in 2015 a study was undertaken by Haeyen, van Hooren and Hutschemaekers (2015) to identify the possible effects of art therapy, focusing on groups of adults with personality disorders. Cathy A. Malchiodi summarised the findings in a *Psychology Today* post titled 'Why Art Therapy Works' (2016). Here, I have highlighted those findings that resonate with what I have experienced when using art in coaching.

- Individuals report that art expression had helped them to stay in the present moment.
- Art made emotions visible, allowing them to further investigate feelings and thoughts.
- Conflicting images could be brought together in one coherent image, something that is often impossible to do with words alone.
- Individuals reported that art expression helped them to put their emotions and non-verbal experiences into words.
- Both creating and looking at what was created supported insight and comprehension of emotions and thoughts and behaviours, and provided a better understanding of experience through the facilitation of the art therapist.

Exploring further, I came across art therapist Liesl Silverstone, the founder of the Person-Centred Art Therapy Centre. In Silverstone's words: 'In my ideal world imaging with the use of art – in fact a wide range of non-verbal creative modes – would be part of learning programmes in the field of human development, resulting in more rounded professionals and thus, in their more balanced, enriched practice' (1997, p. 118). For me, it shows that art therapy is growing in its reach – that there is a recognition that art takes people beyond just healing, giving them many other benefits for personal growth.

The approach

Learning how art therapists manage their sessions, and in particular Leisl Silverstone's person-centred approach, gave me a starting point for bringing art into a coaching session and how to manage myself when facilitating the exploration of a client's art. With experience I have been able to evolve this approach as it relates to coaching, and this is the approach I have set out in this book.

I was particularly drawn to Liesl Silverstone's approach as I am a person-centred coach and it has given me three fundamental areas that form part of my practice today. The first is being truly person-centred (see the work of Carl Rogers, 1902–1987), being non-directive and working based on the belief that the person knows best, that the individual can reach their own potential when working in a climate of genuineness, acceptance and empathy. This is crucial as a coach's role is to facilitate a person's own exploration of their image and not to interpret or offer suggestions. Rather, we are building a connection between our client and their image, holding up a mirror. This is not new for us as coaches and it has been useful to see how and why it is so important for working with art. It provided me with a starting point to think about how to approach and hold the space for art in coaching.

The second was just noticing – noticing everything about the creative process and staying in that space for as long as needed for the person to feel they had explored and understood their image as much as they could at that time. It alerted me to the importance of creating the right space and ensuring there is enough time for the process.

The third was creating a reflective space to begin the imaging process – allowing the hidden and the unconscious to come to the fore so it could have a 'voice' through the image. This led me to exploring mindfulness and the experience of flow. However, I also noted that creating a reflective space didn't always work and that other approaches to imaging could work as effectively.

What happens?

Through my research and my own experience of art therapy I had a wealth of information about what can actually happen in an art therapy session. This then gave me insights into what may happen in a coaching session. This was not only confidence building, but, more importantly, it helped with the contracting process. For example, knowing this approach goes very deep and can bring out hidden material that clients may not be aware of, may not be ready to know or even want to know enabled me to explain the depth of the approach and let clients decide if or how they wanted to proceed. I have since been able to experience what happens in coaching, crafting the approach as it relates to the coaching space.

The most useful insights I had are:

- the ability for art to take someone to a deeper level of awareness
- that it is a very emotional experience
- that meaning can take time to emerge for the client
- that the visual images created can lead to themes and patterns emerging within and between images, as well as across the programme, leading to new discoveries

Going very deep

The ability for this approach to go to deep places is one of the reasons why it is so effective. However, as previously mentioned, using art and facilitating someone else's exploration of their image can unexpectedly take your client to hidden memories and experiences they weren't expecting or are not ready for. It is well known that this approach connects to the unconscious but, in coaching, these may be places we are not skilled or qualified to work in. Likewise, our clients may not want to go there, or something inadvertently gets unlocked that is not helpful for our client at that time. This means that the way we contract for and manage art in coaching sessions is very important. Being able to explain what could happen and that the client has complete control of what happens is crucial for building trust and managing the boundaries of this approach. It is also very important to use it with clear and positive intent. That is, we know exactly why we are using this approach. For example, rather than asking someone to draw whatever is on their mind, which is open and could lead anywhere, we may ask someone to draw what is on their mind specifically in relation to the coaching goal, giving it a clear boundary.

An emotional experience

One of the key purposes of art therapy is emotional exploration. Therefore, this approach connects us to our emotions, and as such it can both enable exploration of emotions as well as unearth emotions. This is something I have experienced in the majority of my sessions, and my clients have been surprised, either by the fact they have had an emotional response, or by how strong their emotional response has been. Some of my clients have been happy to explore their emotions, whilst some have not wanted to talk about it. This links back to the point above, and it is important that clients know that they can choose not to talk about something if they do not want to. As coaches, it means we have to feel confident working in an emotional space. It is working in this emotional space that leads to deeper understanding and awareness.

Meaning may emerge later

When coaching, we often work in a way that helps people work things out in a session or gets them to a point where they feel able to work on it, reflect on it or explore it after the session. With art this is not always the case. It was interesting to note that images can get created and the client may not have a clue as to what they mean, and, importantly, that this is okay as meaning emerges when it is ready to emerge. This has been important to know for managing myself in the coaching space. When someone can't connect to an image there can be a desire to help by providing your own interpretations. However, once your own interpretations are out there, there is no way of knowing how much you have influenced the meaning that subsequently emerges for your client. Being comfortable in a space of not knowing can be hard, but it reinforces the need to be wholly person-centred and to allow someone's meaning to emerge in its own time. I have experienced this for myself when drawing an image whose meaning I did not know. Then, a week later, when doing something completely different, I suddenly realised what it was. It was a wonderful moment! My clients have also experienced this, and meanings have emerged days, weeks or even months later; when they do, it is accompanied by very empowering feelings. Images keep on giving.

Themes

When we coach, we note themes and patterns that arise from our coaching conversations and bring these in as part of the rich data we offer our clients. Using art takes this to another level as a collection of images come together over the sessions that allow side-by-side review. By comparing images over time, key themes may emerge that take the conversation and exploration further. These may be the images themselves, but can also be themes of colour, texture, size, relationships between images, a recurring image or continual use of a particular medium. In my own work, for example, I had a recurring colour – green – which turned out to be a nurturing colour, which was really important to me. With my coaching clients I have had conversations about the colour orange and its links to India, circles and the protective mechanism of armadillos, and I have explored recurring images of water with a client that led to the realisation that they have had a shift from fear to joy.

****

Exploring art therapy has told me a lot about the benefits an art-based approach can bring to coaching, but coaching with art can elicit some unhelpful perceptions and barriers. To help overcome these I turned to the field of neuroscience and, in particular, research into the functions of the brain hemispheres known as hemispheric lateralisation. This is a fascinating area that seems to provide some exciting explanations as to why coaching with art works the way it does. In the next chapter, I explore this in more detail and provide client case study examples to demonstrate the importance of working with, and giving voice to, the right hemisphere.

References

Haeyen, Suzanne, van Hooren, Susan and Hutschemaekers, Giel (2015). 'Perceived Effects of Art Therapy in the Treatment of Personality Disorders, Cluster B/C: A Qualitative Study'. *The Arts in Psychotherapy*, vol. 45 (September): pp. 1–10.
Malchiodi, Cathy A. (2007). *The Art Therapy Sourcebook*. New York: McGraw-Hill.
Malchiodi, Cathy A. (2016). 'Why Art Therapy Works'. *Psychology Today*, August 30. Retrieved from www.psychologytoday.com/gb/blog/arts-and-health/201608/why-art-therapy-works.
McLeod, Saul (2007). 'Carl Rogers'. *Simply Psychology*. Retrieved from www.simplypsychology.org/carl-rogers.html.
Silverstone, Liesl (1997). *Art Therapy The Person-Centred Way – Art and Development of the Person (2nd Edition)*. London: Jessica Kingsley.

Chapter 4

Art and the brain hemispheres

> *'Our talent for division, for seeing the parts, is of staggering importance – second only to our capacity to transcend it, in order to see the whole.'*
> Iain McGilchrist, The Master and His Emissary

Art is a powerful way of communicating, and art therapy together with my own experience has shown me the many benefits art can bring to coaching. Qualitative research in this area has only just started and supporting evidence seems mainly to come from experience and anecdotal evidence. I know it works, and others who use art in a helping way also know it works, but art is a funny thing. Our attitudes towards art, as I explore in Chapter 5, create strong barriers to working in this way and to get over those barriers I wanted to see if there was other research that would support it.

The relatively new field of neuroscience is giving us many insights as to why coaching approaches may work the way they do, and this research is not only informing our practice, but helping to shape it too. It therefore made sense to look to neuroscience to see if it could offer anything that would help.

Building on my own curiosity around the right hemisphere, I was particularly drawn to the research into hemispherical lateralisation, the functions of the right and left hemispheres, and what it was about coaching with art that seemed particularly related to right-hemisphere functions.

However, it is important not to oversimplify hemispherical functional difference, as the brain is a highly complex organ. Both hemispheres are involved in almost all brain functions as the left and right hemispheres are connected by a thick nerve cable, the corpus callosum, through which information is constantly being passed. However, there are some functional differences between the hemispheres that I have found intriguing.

There are also many myths and misconceptions around the right and left hemispheres and you may be wondering if I am linking art-based coaching and the right hemisphere together because the right hemisphere has become known as the creative brain. This is not the case. There is far more to the functions of the two hemispheres than the stereotypical views that have become popularised. Through many decades of research by neuroscientists, we now have much greater insights into the hemispheres' respective functions and their importance in how we experience and process the world around us.

My own curiosity about the brain hemispheres started with Betty Edwards' book *The New Drawing on the Right Side of the Brain* (2001) where Edwards summarised the latest research as part of her research into drawing. This was then further fuelled by Iain McGilchrist's book *The Master and His Emissary* (2012) about the social, political and philosophical implications of the right- and left-hemisphere functions, and left-hemisphere dominance in particular.

McGilchrist looks at the hemispheres from the point of view that they create for us two different realities that are opposed to each other. Although they co-operate to create the recognisable world in which we live, there is also a conflict and a power struggle between them. This struggle seems to mirror the conflicts that our clients can experience. For example, when clients are stuck in thinking loops and behaviour patterns, it as though their left hemisphere is dominating. Then, when they make that insight that enables them to see things in a way that leads to positive change, their right hemisphere has come in with something new. The client seems to be moving from their dominant left hemisphere's reality, to opening up to the possibilities of their right hemisphere's reality. This also starts to explain the effectiveness of coaching with art, as it helps clients tap into another way of seeing their world: the right-hemisphere world.

Research into the functions of the brain hemispheres

The different workings of the two hemispheres, together with the importance and function of the corpus callosum, was initially discovered through the Nobel Prize-winning work of Roger W. Sperry and his students in the 1970s at the California Institute of Technology. Sperry was working with people who suffered from severe epilepsy and, to try and alleviate the severe symptoms of his patients, he severed their corpus callosum. In so doing he discovered that a main function of the corpus callosum was to provide communication between the two hemispheres to allow transmission of memory and learning. He also discovered that the two brain halves continued to function independently. This led him to do more in-depth research into this area. Since then, neuroscientist Michael Gazzaniga, a student of Perry's, and many others have continued the work with split-brain patients through to the present day.

In addition to split-brain studies, there have been studies undertaken with people who have suffered strokes in one or the other of the hemispheres, or where people have damaged right or left hemispheres through accidents. Nowadays, neuroscientists can work with normal-functioning brains by temporarily disabling one or the other hemisphere for a moment through techniques such as the Wada test, which allows the neuroscientist to look at language and memory on one side of the brain at a time. Now it is also possible to use brain

Table 4.1 Left-hemisphere and right-hemisphere functions and differences

Left mode		Right mode	
Virtual	Re-presenting that which the right hemisphere experiences. Paying attention to the world it has created. It is self-consistent, self-contained and disconnected from that which is outside ourselves	**Reality**	All new experience is perceived here first. Paying attention to that which exists apart from ourselves
Consistent	Seeing things in relation to what it already knows and supressing data that it believes is currently not relevant	**Change**	Experiencing the world around us in constant change with no one experience being the same as the next. For example, a river in constant flow, always the same but not the same. More capable of a frame shift
Parts	Breaking things down into units and categorising, labelling, naming and isolating things. Creates a whole by putting units together	**Whole**	Seeing things as a whole, in context, both spatially and the betweeness of/relationships of things. Noticing the peripheral
Vocal	Where speech resides	**Silent**	Has a vocabulary but is reliant on the left hemisphere to deliver it. Making the perceptual links between words; the home of metaphor. Specialising in non-verbal communication such as face recognition
Impersonal	Attending to superficial social emotions	**Personal**	Giving emotional value and attending to unconscious emotional processing. The source of our moral sense and where empathy resides. Feeling emotions through our body. Maintaining a coherent and continuous unified sense of self (narrative).
Analytic	Figuring things out step-by-step and part-by-part. Creating rules. Likes certainty	**Synthetic**	Seeing things as a whole and how they work together, the connectedness of things. Comfortable with paradox and complexity

Logical and linear	Drawing conclusions based on logic: one thing following another in logical order. Focusing on the explicit. Drawing conclusions based on logic, reason and facts – a linear sequential argument. Thinking in terms of linked ideas, one thought directly following another, often leading to a convergent conclusion	**Intuitive and deductive**	Making leaps of insight, often based on patterns, hunches, feelings or visual images. Not requiring a basis of reason or facts; has a willingness to suspend judgements; deducing. Seeing whole things all at once; perceiving the overall patterns and structures, often leading to divergent conclusions. Where the aha! moment resides
Symbolic	Using a symbol to stand for something. For example, the drawn form of the eye stands for the eye, the + sign stands for the process of addition	**Actual**	Relating to things as they are, in the present moment
Abstract	Taking out small bits of information and using them to represent the whole thing	**Real**	Seeing likenesses among things; understanding metaphoric relationships. Doing nothing in abstract
Temporal	Keeping track of time, sequencing one thing after another; doing first things first, second things second etc.	**Non-temporal**	Perceiving time as one continual flow, with no beginning or end – a feeling of being without a sense of time

Sources: Table developed from McGilchrist (2012) and Edwards (2001).

It should be noted that any binary construct like this table is essentially a left-hemisphere way of doing things and, whilst helpful, can miss some of the complexity.

imaging processes where neuroscientists can literally see which parts of the brain activate when people perform functions or are exposed to experiences.

This research has shown that each half of the brain has different capabilities, and that both are involved in higher cognitive functioning and, although complimentary, have their own ways of perceiving reality. Jerre Levy, in her doctoral studies in the 1970s, showed that the right hemisphere processes in a way that is rapid, complex, global, spatial and perceptual – processing that is different from, although comparable in complexity to, the left hemisphere. Levy also found that the two modes of processing tend to interfere with each other, preventing maximum performance. It can literally mean that the right hand doesn't know what the left hand is doing! (Edwards, 2001, pp. 32–33.) In addition, the California Institute of Technology found evidence that the right, non-speaking half of the brain experiences, responds

The two hemispheres of the brain

The brain has two halves, the right and the left, and they are connected by a thick nerve cable called the corpus callosum. This nerve cable allows the hemispheres to share as well as inhibit information from each other.

The halves are asymmetric, with the left being wider at the back and extending further back a little under the right hemisphere and the right extending further forward, overlapping a little on the left. Neuroscientists refer to this as the Yakovlevian torque.

The functions of the hemispheres cross over. That is, the right hemisphere manages our left side and the left hemisphere manages our right side. For example, the left hand is managed by the right hemisphere, whereas the right hand is managed by the left hemisphere.

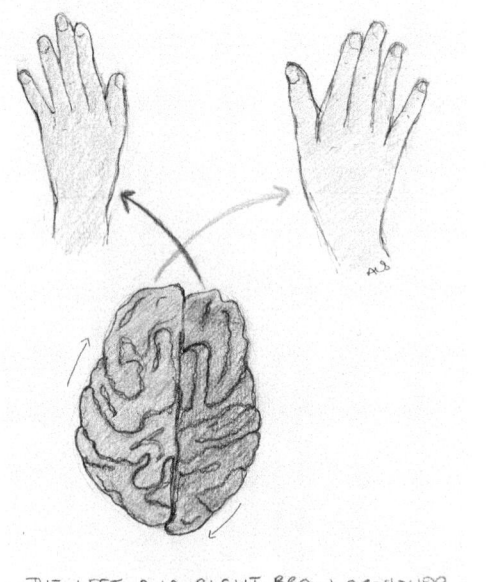

Figure 4.1 The left- and right-hemisphere crossover; illustration by the author

with feelings and processes information on its own. However, in individuals with intact brains, the vocal left half of the brain dominates most of the time.

Most recently, psychiatrist Ian McGilchrist, in the first part of his book *The Master and His Emissary*, brings together much of the research and thinking around the brain hemispheres. McGilchrist focuses on the different ways the hemispheres analyse and perceive the world through the nature of the attention they give. He explains that all new experience comes to the right hemisphere first, and then when it is familiar enough it passes to the left hemisphere, which then re-presents it. As a result, the left hemisphere's attention is generally narrow and focused, where it sees things 'abstracted from context, and broken into parts, from which it reconstructs a "whole"' (2012, p. 27). On the other hand, the right hemisphere's attention 'is broad and vigilant', seeing things 'as a whole, and in their context' (*ibid.*), and aware of the relationships between and around things.

I have found McGilchrist's book enormously helpful in understanding the different functions of the hemispheres and the research and experiments carried out to support the findings.

Hemisphere function and coaching with art

Both brain hemispheres have many functions; in his book, McGilchrist (2012) dedicates over 60 pages to exploring these functions and the differences between the left and right hemispheres. There is so much rich information in his second chapter that I would have loved to repeat it here. However, this is not possible so here I have highlighted and summarised those passages I found particularly interesting in trying to understand why coaching with art is so powerful. I am mindful that editing in this way may not give all the complexity to the hemispheres' functions and if this is an area that interests you, I encourage you to explore further.

Whilst my focus is on the right hemisphere, I don't want to lessen the extraordinary importance of the left hemisphere. The left hemisphere gives us, amongst other things, the ability for reason and logic that makes us uniquely human. It has enabled us to expand our knowledge and capability in a way that is quite breath-taking and has made the world we live in today. However, in the context of coaching, the dominant vocal left hemisphere can also bring with it some challenges, particularly for the silent right hemisphere. Therefore, when exploring right-hemisphere functions, I have also highlighted left-hemisphere functions that can bring a challenge to accessing the right hemisphere's experiences and perceptions. Understanding this challenge has also helped me further understand why coaching with art works so well, as the approach I take actively encourages the left hemisphere to relinquish its dominance, allowing for right-hemisphere-mode working.

To bring the research to life, I have included case study excerpts, as appropriate, to demonstrate these different functions as they happen in practice.

The functions I am exploring are:

- working with the whole, as it really is, in all its complexity
- metaphor
- frame shifts
- understanding the true narrative
- the aha! moment and transformational shift
- emotional value and complexity
- giving the silent right hemisphere a voice

Working with the whole, as it really is, in all its complexity[1]

The first area I want to explore is seeing the world as a whole versus seeing the world in parts.

The right hemisphere sees things as a whole, as they are, in context both spatially and in the relationships between things. It sees how things are connected to other things around them, and how they work together with those things around them. The right hemisphere has a holistic and Gestalt perception of the world. This function also means that the right hemisphere is comfortable with complexity and paradox as it can hold whatever it perceives as a whole, without the need to analyse or rationalise.

Famous puzzle images, such as the Rubin vase (where a viewer can simultaneously see a vase and two faces), demonstrate our right hemisphere's capacity for being comfortable with, and holding, paradox.

The left hemisphere, on the other hand, has the function of breaking things down into parts and units. It categorises, names, labels and isolates things. This is extraordinarily important, as it is through this function that the left hemisphere gives us a stable world. (I explore this more when looking at frame shifts later in the chapter.) However, as a result of breaking things down, it then creates a whole by putting the units together. The downside to this is it can end up failing to achieve the whole as it really is. In addition, it can take out small bits of information and use them to represent the whole thing. For example, when we draw the symbol of a 'stick man', we use it to represent the whole person – male or female.

As a result of its function of creating a stable world, the left hemisphere creates and needs certainty. It is not comfortable with complexity and paradox.

To experience the ability of the right hemisphere to see things as a whole versus the left hemisphere's ability for trying to build a whole from parts, and the challenge this brings for communication and understanding, try the following spiral staircase exercise. I use this in my workshops and continual professional development (CPD) events as a way of demonstrating the parts-versus-the-whole difference between the hemispheres.

Puzzle image

What do you see?

Figure 4.2 Drawn by the author, based on a drawing by E.G. Boring (1930), taken from a German postcard from 1888

You may see an old woman, you may see a young woman or you may be able to see both and not be at all concerned about it. If it is the latter, this is the right hemisphere in action, holding the paradox. Usually, we will initially see one, and have to 'look' for the other. At first, this can feel a little uncomfortable, but then the right hemisphere enables us to say 'it's okay, it's both!'

The spiral staircase exercise

Sit on your hands; when you are comfortable, describe a spiral staircase. Try not to move, just describe it verbally. You may find this quite difficult! You may find yourself using words to describe parts of the staircase, building up a picture from units to create a whole image. You may relate it to similar objects to help describe it. Your left hemisphere is trying to build the whole from parts, or trying to find objects that have some similarity. Your left hemisphere doesn't have the words for it and struggles to describe it. In the meantime, you may be finding it really hard to keep your hands still. You may even find yourself making head or whole-body movements to describe it. This is because the vocal left hemisphere, where speech resides, is trying to find the words to describe the staircase, and the silent right hemisphere is trying to come in and use non-verbal communication to help.

Now release your hands, and describe a spiral staircase. You can do this within seconds and it is a full description using the visual imagery of your hands (non-vocal right hemisphere) as well as words (vocal left hemisphere). Your right hemisphere has visually and spatially described it very effectively, very quickly and as a whole. The left hemisphere labels it, but it is the right hemisphere that accurately portrays it. As McGilchrist says (2012, p. 93), 'our talent for division, for seeing the parts, is of staggering importance – second only to our capacity to transcend it, in order to see the whole'.

Figure 4.3 Spiral staircase; illustration by the author

When describing the spiral staircase with your hands, it can feel as though you are experiencing it and knowing it by being 'in' the spiral staircase. You just know it and experience it. This is the right-hemisphere experience.

When working with our clients we are often working with quite complex, and sometimes paradoxical, issues. For example, clients may be working with emotional and relational complexity; they may be managing conflicting values or the tensions between 'shoulds' and 'oughts'. Being able to work with these complexities is extremely important if clients are to be able to make sense of and move through them positively. However, these complexities and paradoxes can often be difficult to articulate and work with. Clients can be lost for words, explaining they just 'know', but can't describe; they may be able to tell us what it feels like but can't analyse it. The right hemisphere cannot communicate because it doesn't have the words, and the left hemisphere may also be actively suppressing the data because it wants to maintain certainty. If we want to break through this, we need to work with the right hemisphere and encourage the left hemisphere to relinquish control.

When coaching with art, I have found that a client's image making process allows them to externalise the complexity of their whole experience into a safe space (the visually created space) and, by so doing, makes it easier for them to explore and understand it.

Using art is an embodied experience and replicates the right hemisphere's ability to see things as a whole, in context, with all the complexity and paradox that may be within. Once externalised into the created visual image, the client can then reflect and explore with curiosity, taking as long as they need to find their own meaning and understanding within it.

Coaching with art example: working with the whole

A great example of this was in my first coaching session with Sam. Sam was exploring her role in the professional organisation she had recently joined as a director. Sam had been recruited to bring about change and introduce best practice. In her image (Colour Image 1, plate section), Sam captured the situation for herself – not only the organisation, but how she felt, the tensions within the organisation around change and the complexity of the relationships within it. Sam described the green circle with the round flowers within it as representing the organisation and the different ornamentations on the flowers representing different variations within the profession. The blue roots coming from the flowers extending just beyond the green circle symbolised the potential for growth in the organisation. Sam, although from the same profession, showed herself as a purple circle pushing its way in to the green circle. The additional images relate to the organisation's structure, with the organisational hierarchy representing those from the profession in green and those not in purple.

Sam describes the image as 'a depiction of the tension between growth and constraint, between innovation and reservation, that seemed to be a unifying theme across the issues I had been contemplating earlier, although I hadn't recognised it as such at that point'. By externalising the whole issue into one image, giving Sam the space to explore the complexities within it, she was able to understand what was going on for her. It also allowed for deeper awareness – 'It was a revelation to me that I still felt an outsider in this job' – leading to an exploration of difference in later sessions.

Metaphor[2]

Through the right-hemisphere function of seeing and perceiving experience as a whole, the right hemisphere is also the home of metaphoric thinking. This is because metaphoric thinking is a way of expressing our emotions and experience as a whole, all at once. Metaphors encapsulate in one word or one phrase the entirety of an experience or idea. For example, 'I can see the light at the end of the tunnel' is often used as a metaphor for hope, or 'I can't see the wood for the trees' when we can't find the meaning or answer, or 'a lightbulb moment' when we experience a flash of insight!

We use metaphor every day and it allows us to create verbally an image of what we are feeling and experiencing. Our metaphors can describe a depth of feeling and complexity that helps us make sense of the world and helps others to understand us, and us to understand them. McGilchrist (2012, p. 155, n. 2) says that metaphor is the function of the right hemisphere, which gives us the link between language and the world it refers to – that 'it can reach outside the system of signs to life itself'.

The imagery used in metaphor is figurative, that is, it is of an image of something we know and can visualise, for example, 'I feel as though I have the world on my shoulders'. However, when working with art in coaching I have noticed that although, by its very process, it works in a metaphorical way, it goes far beyond the verbal figurative metaphor.

Whilst the imagery that my clients create can come from a metaphorical guided exercise such as 'there is a box in front of you and inside the box is everything that is important to you. Now open the box and rummage around. What do you find?', most of the time I create a space for a client's own image to emerge that has meaning to them. These images aren't just representational; they are often very abstract and, often, the more abstract they are, the richer they become.

In addition, the metaphor isn't just the image, it is everything about the image. The colour, the relationships between the forms within it and other aspects of the image such as the texture, the weight of the line, the materials used and so on.

This language of the image is also the language that most often gets used when referring back to an image, to a session, to an insight, because it captures the entire meaning.

Coaching with art works very closely with the right hemisphere's capacity for metaphorical thinking and seems to go deeper.

Coaching with art example: metaphor

In Sam's second session, she had wanted to capture the image of a slinky toy, but had unconsciously drawn a curl (Colour Image 2, plate section). Sam says about this image: 'What I have drawn to represent me is a blonde curl and the curl is very clearly a metaphor for my "otherness"'. We spoke about the size, shape and colours of the curl: 'The colours are bright, strong and multi-dimensional, and that towards the end I added some flashes of a bright yellow in spaces that had been darker earlier in the evolution of the image... Although not entirely round, the image of the curl is round in shape, with soft borders.'

Sam talked about the complexity of her feelings and of being a mix of contradictions. This was represented in her image through the different textures of paint and pastels and the different colours Sam had used. Sam described the orange as bright, unusual, warm and playful and the pink as warmer, stating that this (all the colours and the curl) represented her.

Frame shifts[3]

The ability for us to experience frame shifts lies with the right hemisphere.

McGilchrist (2012) explains that all our new experience comes to our right hemisphere first and then, once it is familiar enough, it is passed to our left hemisphere, where it is processed, analysed and re-presented. By doing this, the left hemisphere creates a stable world for us to live in – a world that we can build on, come to 'know' and do things with. It does this by categorising, labelling and isolating things. In addition, it also creates rules. For example, if we take a river, the reality is that from one moment to the next a river is never the same. Water is in constant motion; surface patterns change all the time and the river's shape will be constantly changing as its banks are eroded or silt deposits are laid down. Also, one river is not the same as another. This constant change and uniqueness of things is what the right hemisphere experiences. However, our left hemisphere has given us the label 'river', and with that label comes certain 'rules' that enable us to apply that label to other things we experience that fit those rules. We can live comfortably with the fact that the river is in constant change because we have stabilised it into the concept of a river, and it doesn't matter that one river is not the same as another as long as it fits the rule; they are all rivers. It would be a challenging world to live in if everything we encountered was completely, unpredictably new and unforeseen!

The left-hemisphere function of creating a stable world means it focuses on what it knows and creates rules that need to be followed. As a result, it can actively ignore data it believes is not relevant to or does not fit those rules. It also means it is unlikely to be open to something new or something different, and is more likely to keep people stuck in thinking loops.

On the other hand, because the right hemisphere is open to the new and experiences things in constant flow, it is open to the peripheral and to thinking outside the box. It is therefore more capable of a frame shift, helping people move out of those thinking loops.

McGilchrist also explains that the right hemisphere will come up with a number of different solutions which can all be held and explored, without rushing to settle on one. By contrast, the left hemisphere will focus on the one that fits best with what it already knows and will tend to stick with it.

When coaching, we know the importance and power of frame shifts to enable our clients to make positive and lasting changes. Therefore, to give greater opportunity for frame shifts, it makes sense to be coaching in a way that allows our clients to access their right hemisphere's perceptions and experiences of the world.

Coaching with art clearly works with the right hemisphere. It gives the right hemisphere a voice. It also actively quietens the left hemisphere, allowing for more right-hemisphere perceptions to come to the fore and increasing the opportunities for frame shifts.

Coaching with art example: frame shifts

Nearly all my coaching sessions have had within them frameshifts. These aren't necessarily the aha! moment; they are opportunities to see something new, something different that shifts a client's thinking, changes their perception and allows them to move forward.

For example, when Amelia was exploring her new relationship, she drew a picture that in the session raised lots of questions for her (Colour Image 3, plate section). After the session, she had the following insight: 'Somehow, as I look at the picture again. . . those figures each feel strong in themselves, firmly grounded, standing strong in themselves, yet connected in a very loving way. Maybe that's the reason that I didn't paint them too close together?'

The image making process and exploration enabled Amelia to see the relationship from a different perspective. A frame shift.

Understanding the true narrative[4]

Here, I want to explore the left hemisphere challenge of maintaining a stable world and what that means for getting to the truth of the matter when coaching.

As we have already seen when talking about frame shifts, the left hemisphere creates for us a stable world, but it also has a role in maintaining that consistent and stable world. We have also seen that the left hemisphere may actively suppress data that doesn't fit with its rules. In addition, research shows that the left hemisphere can also suppress the right hemisphere's data, or leap in with explanations of its own, so that we stay comfortable and certain – but perhaps wrong! Neuroscientist Michael Gazzaniga identified this function through his split-brain-patient studies, calling it 'the left-brain interpreter'. Studies have since shown that the left-brain interpreter applies to everyday behaviour in the general population.

To demonstrate the left-brain interpreter, I have summarised below the well-known experiment that Gazzaniga and LeDoux performed when discovering this concept (Gazzaniga, 1998, pp. 51–55).

The chicken claw experiment

Here, Gazzaniga and LeDoux show how the left hemisphere can come in with its own explanations of what the right hemisphere is doing. They also show that the right hemisphere can easily communicate through visual imagery.

In this experiment a split-brain patient (someone who has had their corpus callosum severed so that the two halves of the brain cannot communicate with each other) is shown a picture projected to one or the other hemisphere only, and is asked to pick a card connected with the scene and not to speak. Speaking is a left-hemisphere activity.

In one example they show a snow scene to the patient's right hemisphere by showing it only to his left eye. They then ask him to choose an appropriate picture from an array of cards, with either hand. He cannot say what it is that he has seen because the right hemisphere cannot speak, but he is able with his left hand to go straight to the picture of a shovel. (The left hand, like the left eye, is managed by the right hemisphere.) However, since the left hemisphere did not see anything as the right eye wasn't shown anything, his right hand chooses at random and only by chance may pick up a card of relevance. (The right hand, like the right eye, is managed by the left hemisphere.)

They then show a picture of a snow scene to his right hemisphere (left eye) and at the same time show a picture of a chicken claw to his left hemisphere (right eye). Each hemisphere has knowledge of only one picture and each is different. The hemispheres cannot communicate with each other because the patient's corpus callosum has been severed.

Without speaking, he is asked to choose an appropriate card. The left hand (right hemisphere) again chooses a shovel because the right hemisphere has seen the snow, but the right hand (left hemisphere) chooses a picture of a chicken because the left hemisphere has seen a picture of a chicken claw.

When asked to say why the left hand (right hemisphere) has chosen a shovel, his verbal left hemisphere, which has to respond to the question but knows nothing of the snow scene (the real reason for choosing the shovel), explains that he saw a chicken and of course chose a shovel because it is needed to clean out the chicken shed.

The authors of this research said that, 'without batting an eye', the left hemisphere draws mistaken conclusions from the information available. They also said that the statement came out as a matter of fact. There was no suggestion of guessing or wondering – 'yet, the left did not offer its suggestion in a guessing vein but rather as a statement of fact' (Gazzaniga and LeDoux, 1978, pp. 148–149).

The left hemisphere had come in with a plausible, if incorrect, reason for the right hemisphere choosing a shovel. It made sense to the narrative that it was giving about the chicken claw.

There are also suggestions that the explanations provided by the left-brain interpreter may also enhance the opinion people have about themselves, producing beliefs which may stop themselves from seeing the reality of the situation, and maintaining patterns of behaviour that may not be helpful (Schacter, 2002).

This ability of the left hemisphere is sometimes called the storytelling brain, as it creates a narrative about our experiences and memories that is coherent, and the coherence is more important than the accuracy! (Gots, 2012.)

Most of the time this difference isn't an issue, but when put together with the other differences being considered here, and in the context of left-hemisphere dominance, it may start to explain why clients can get stuck in thinking loops, maintain unhelpful patterns of behaviour and thinking and not be open to new information. They may be stuck in their left-hemisphere-re-presented world; they may be too focused on what they know, ignoring data that doesn't fit with that model; they can't breakthrough. Here, the left hemisphere needs to relinquish dominance and allow the right hemisphere to come in and communicate the complete and true picture. It seems it is the right hemisphere that helps people get out of unhelpful patterns through deeper awareness and understanding of what the reality of the situation is.

In coaching we often work with clients who want to break out of unhelpful patterns, or who are stuck in thinking loops and can't get beyond them. Working with the right hemisphere gives greater opportunity and possibilities for our clients to see the situation as it really is, which can lead to changes in patterns of thinking and behaviour that ultimately help them achieve their coaching aims.

When using art in coaching I have found it to be a fast and powerful way of helping the truth of the issue emerge, breaking through thinking loops and/or deepening awareness and understanding of unhelpful patterns.

Coaching with art example: understanding the true narrative

A great example of this happened in Keira's session.

I usually start an imaging process using a mindfulness approach to quieten the thinking left-hemisphere and to allow images to emerge in their own time. However, it was clear that Keira wasn't getting very much from these images. Kiera was judging and censoring what she was doing. When reflecting together, Keira said that she was wanting them to be perfect so that she had a really nice image to take away. Keira was clearly overthinking the process and had a set idea of what she wanted to achieve in the session – that it was important to be able to take home a nice piece of art work. Her left hemisphere appeared to be in charge.

Later in the session, to break through this, when Keira was struggling to articulate what was going on for her, I asked her to just draw it, in the moment. This direct in-the-moment approach really worked for her. Keira said that she suddenly felt free and could draw intuitively as there was no preconceived idea about an image. It broke through her thinking loop, allowing her right hemisphere to have a voice. It was these later pictures that gave Keira her shift and aha! Moment, enabling her to consciously understand the truth of what was going on for her. Kiera said that the 'just-draw-it' moment was more direct and intuitive, and really worked. Then, reflecting after the session about the two images she created in the moment. Keira said: 'Both the pictures I really like, and how they speak to you having gone through this process. Amazed you got me to this point. Very powerful' (Colour Images 5 and 6, plate section).

The aha! moment and transformational shift[5]

The aha! moment is probably one of the most well-known right-hemisphere functions and one we often encounter when coaching.

We experience the aha! moment with our clients when they have moments of everything falling in to place without them having to figure things out in a logical order. They just know! It is one of the most powerful aspects of coaching and is the right-hemisphere mode working: the intuitive, subjective, relational, holistic, time-free mode.

The right hemisphere has the aha! moment because it deduces through recognising patterns and making connections, together with feelings and hunches. It also notices the peripheral and that which is just outside of awareness, allowing wider connections to be made. The right hemisphere sees the conclusion as a whole thing all at once, 'just knowing', without reason or facts, giving us insights and the aha! moment.

The left hemisphere, by contrast, is logical and linear and reaches conclusions by linking one idea after another. This is extraordinarily beneficial for the development of our knowledge and the creation of the world we live in. However, when we link this to the left hemisphere's need for consistency, working with rules and focusing on what it knows, the left hemisphere can, in certain circumstances, make incorrect conclusions. We have seen this in Michael Gazzaniga's concept of the left-brain interpreter (above; Gazzaniga, 1998, pp. 51–55).

However, once the person has had the aha! moment, the left hemisphere can then come in with the analysis as the person knows what they want or need to do. The left hemisphere is now working with the new shifted reality.

The great thing about working with art in coaching is that I have noticed it increases the opportunities for transformational shifts to occur.

Coaching with art example: the aha! moment and transformational shift

I have shared here Amelia's transformational shift that happened in our final session together (Colour Image 4, plate section). These are Amelia's own reflections on what she experienced. 'The key moment of this session . . . was the moment that I instinctively and unconsciously started to paint some blue at the bottom-left of the picture. I had no idea why. Then I picked up the brush and added little white wavy lines which then became waves in my mind. It was at that moment that I was struck by a thought that had an almost visceral impact on me. "I want to be with M by the sea". This felt incredibly strong and certain and really took me by surprise! There was an added sense of feeling like I was coming home . . . But actually, on reflection, I think this whole image is a "coming home" for me. Coming home to the real me who has been missing, presumed lost, for a long time. WOW – this is quite a profound realisation. . . Another lightbulb moment: maybe this is the reason that water has been a recurring theme in my images? Not because I'm afraid of it, but because I want to be closer to it?'

Emotional value and complexity[6]

McGilchrist explores the many complexities of the role of the right hemisphere around emotional value and emotional understanding. He explains that the left hemisphere, through breaking things into parts and categorising things, is more impersonal and emotionally neutral. It is also focused on its re-presented world, whereas the right hemisphere is focused on the world around us and is connected to the external world and the people within it, paying attention to the personal. Interestingly, there is one emotion that is more closely linked to the left hemisphere: anger. This may be because in certain moments there is a frustration at some level that the world is not conforming to the left hemisphere's re-presented, analysed perception – that there is a level of outrage that the left hemisphere's way of experiencing the world is being challenged, particularly as it tends to believe it is right!

To be able to fully understand ourselves, we need to be able to connect with, value and understand our emotions and emotional responses. We also need to be able to understand and value the emotions of others if we are to build successful relationships and be part of society. In coaching, working at an emotional level enables our clients to make a deeper level of connection and understand what is really going on for them. The right hemisphere is central for us to be able to do this, and I have highlighted here some of those key emotional right-hemisphere functions and capabilities that support this.

- The right hemisphere holds emotional memories.
- The right hemisphere is more associated with the recall of memories associated with personal meaning.
- Empathy resides with the right hemisphere as it is connected to the world outside of ourselves.
- The right hemisphere gives us emotional value.
- The right hemisphere is more closely involved with unconscious emotional processing through the right amygdala.
- The right hemisphere has an affinity with bodily experience, as we experience the world through all of our senses and we experience emotions through our bodies. All new experience comes to the right hemisphere first.

Art in all its forms – both ancient and modern – is an expression of not only what artists want to say, but also how they feel. We also respond to art we encounter in an emotional way.

When coaching with art, we are not only giving the right hemisphere a voice, but we are working in a very physical way. The physicality of art is one of the ways personal expression is conveyed and seems to be one of the reasons why it works at such a deeply emotional level. For example, when watching clients create pieces of work, they will often stand or sit on the floor, and use their whole bodies, not just their hands. When using the materials, you can see their wrists, arms, shoulders all moving; they may change the way they stand and sometimes the whole body moves in the direction of the marks they make. As James said in one of his sessions: 'I selected watercolour sticks and started by making a spirally flower design from the centre of the page, noticing as I did so how one draws with one's whole body.' James later reflected: 'Art is physical and I have been aware of how my body has been engaged in the exercises, and this has spoken to me.'

Emotional expression also comes through the colours that are used, the type of medium used, the size of an image, the texture created and the varying pressure applied to the marks made.

Clients can find working with emotions quite hard, often finding it difficult to identify and describe them. Emotions can often be complex and clients may be wary of exploring emotions as they may feel exposed and vulnerable. There may also be societal or cultural aspects at play. As a result, clients can gloss over or explain away their emotions. Working with art, as previously explained, holds complexity, which includes emotional complexity, and it does so in a safe space within the visual image created. This then allows the client, and coach, to hold those emotions and just be with them.

By giving the right hemisphere its voice through art, we can provide a richer and deeper conversation about the emotional truth of things, which in turn enables the client to have a greater understanding of their values, belief systems, motivators and drivers as well as their personal narratives.

Coaching with art example: emotional value and complexity

In all the case studies in this book, as well as many experiences in the workshops, people being coached have had emotional responses. Some of those responses have been very strong and transformational, others have been puzzling and reflective. As one participant in a workshop said after exploring an image they had created 'it emotionally took me by surprise'.

It is also important to note that whilst most have been open to exploring their (sometimes unexpected) emotional responses, some have not. It is important to respect this as this approach can take people to places they don't want to go to or are not ready to go to. I talk more about this and other boundaries we need to manage and be aware of when working in this way in the 'how-to' part of the book.

In all the examples provided so far, the emotional complexity is there. Whether it is Sam holding the tensions of change or her feelings of 'otherness', Amelia's desert island and the exploration of her new relationship, Keira's breakthrough images and the feeling of being free, or Amelia's aha! image and that powerful visceral feeling that came with it. All have emotional complexity within them. All have been able to hold that complexity, explore it in their own time and move forward with it.

As Sam said at the end of her first session: 'I still find it completely fascinating that these truths have emerged so quickly and profoundly, enabling me to articulate what have until now been nothing more than gut feelings.'

Giving the silent right hemisphere a voice

One of the most well-known differences between the hemispheres is that of speech, and it is perhaps one of the most obvious reasons why coaching with art works so effectively.

The right hemisphere is silent as the function for vocalised speech lies with the left hemisphere. Both hemispheres have language and both play a role in the function of language, but the silent right hemisphere is reliant on the vocal left hemisphere to speak on its behalf.

As mentioned earlier, the hemispheres can actively interfere with each other and the left hemisphere can suppress right-hemisphere data if it doesn't fit with what it knows, doesn't fit with its logical and linear approach to decision making or doesn't help create a consistent and comfortable world for us. This can pose a problem for the silent right hemisphere and for us. You may have experienced this issue both for yourself and with your clients. Have you ever tried to remember something, such as a word, a name or a pin code, and it only comes to you when you are doing something completely different, when you have stopped 'thinking' about it? By doing something different, it would seem you are distracting the left hemisphere from the task and allowing the right hemisphere to come in and solve it for you. This is a mini aha! moment.

We may experience this with clients who are going around in circles and can't seem to make those shifts in their thinking and perceptions that would help them move forward. Perhaps you may have experienced clients who just can't 'see the wood for the trees'. Others may have an inkling, a feeling about something, but can't articulate what that something is. Other phrases you may have heard are 'I just know but I can't explain it', 'I know there is something, but I just don't know what', 'I can tell you what it isn't'. These situations may be accompanied by heightened emotions such as frustration, exasperation, sadness and defeatism.

All of these scenarios suggest there is something going on that cannot be communicated, that the right hemisphere may have some useful information to share, but the left hemisphere doesn't have the words for it, may be suppressing it or ignoring it – and can't or won't vocalise it. This isn't helped by the fact that the vocal left hemisphere is dominant most of the time.

So, when we want to explore at a deeper level of awareness and access that which is hard to express, or perhaps even not known, we need to work in a way that enables the left hemisphere to relinquish the task and allow the right hemisphere to do it. We need to do it in a way that gives the right hemisphere a voice so it can communicate its perceptions.

I have found that coaching with art can be very effective in quieting the left hemisphere and allowing the right hemisphere to take charge. I hope you have been able to see this demonstrated through the examples provided above, showing how the image making process externalises and makes visible the right hemisphere's experiences and perceptions. The art my clients create gives their right hemisphere a voice through not only the image, but also the language of the image making process. This enables them to access the non-verbal, unconscious parts of their internal world. It enables them to externalise the complex, the paradoxical and the hidden. They are able to hold the whole just as it is, in all its complexity.

Coaching with art has also given my clients a safe space to explore their emotional complexity and, by so doing, it has given them the space to start connecting to, reflecting on and understanding what is going on for them. If I do it right, they talk spontaneously, using right-hemisphere vocabulary; if they don't know what it means, I know this is okay as meaning will come later when it is ready to be known.

Coaching with art example: giving the silent right hemisphere a voice

A great example of quietening the left hemisphere and allowing the right hemisphere to have a voice through visual imagery happened in trio-coaching in a workshop. I was observing from the side when I heard the person being coached say 'I am picking up this blue pencil. I have no idea why I am picking it up, but I need some blue here'. He then scribbled blue marks quite vigorously onto his image. He then said: 'I think I need some of this blue over here' and started to make more tentative marks in a different area of his image. As he was doing this, he had a shift in understanding that enabled him to label it. 'This is values, and we need these values here [pointing at the area with tentative blue marks]. We contracted for the values here, but not here.' The visual image and the image making language enabled him to breakthrough and give meaning to what he was experiencing and understand it.

This also happened with Amelia's aha! image (Colour Image 4, plate section), where she talked about 'instinctively and unconsciously' painting blue and having no idea why, followed by picking up a brush and adding white wavy lines which only then became waves in her mind. It was at that point that meaning emerged for Amelia and she had her aha! moment.

Right-hemisphere time-free mode[7]

To work with the right hemisphere gives richness to our coaching and, if we want to work in this way, it is helpful to know how to recognise when someone has shifted into right-hemisphere mode.

One of the differences between the two hemispheres is that of time and it is this difference, through our response to time, that lets us know if we have shifted to right-hemisphere dominance in that moment.

The left hemisphere works with time by breaking it up into units (minutes, seconds, hours, days, weeks, months etc.) and being consciously aware of it, whereas the right hemisphere experiences it as more of a continual flow, like a river in constant motion.

When we lose track of time (i.e., we are not analysing, measuring and monitoring time), we experience something we often refer to as flow.

Flow was first identified by positive psychologist Mihaly Csikszentmihalyi as an experience that led to greater consciousness and a higher level of achievement (*Psychology Today*, 2016).

When experiencing flow, the person loses a sense of time; they become unaware of and are not interested in what is going on around them. They are fully absorbed and confident in what they are doing. It is a very enjoyable state where the task feels effortless and as though it is being directed by something other than yourself. Whilst flow may be a whole-brain experience, the time-free mode of the right hemisphere is a crucial part of the experience.

When coaching with art my clients often become unaware of the passage of time, wondering where the time went when we come to close a session!

As one participant on a workshop said: 'I felt completely alone whilst I was creating. I was completely absorbed. I did not need to pay attention to the relationship – only to me.'

Quietening the left hemisphere

To be able to work with the right hemisphere, to give it a voice, we have to be able to slow down and quieten the dominant left hemisphere. Sperry's split-brain studies indicated that the dominant left hemisphere prefers not to relinquish tasks unless it really dislikes the job, either because the job takes too much time, is too detailed or too slow. So, we need to work in a way that the left hemisphere will either turn down or will stop interfering with the right hemisphere (Edwards, 2001, p. 46). This can also lead to flow.

Flow comes, according to Csíkszentmihalyi (*Psychology Today*, 2016), when the client is faced with a task that has a clear goal that requires specific and clear responses, and is a challenge that is just about manageable.

When coaching with art, I invite my clients to work in the moment, without censorship and judgement. I work in a way that encourages my clients to trust in their intuition and imagination. I do not ask them to capture what they are 'thinking' because this keeps them in the left-hemisphere space of words and they would end up illustrating a left-hemisphere thought. The task is also clear but often challenging as it takes them outside of their comfort zone; but it is manageable. We can all create imagery that expresses our interior selves.

To quieten the left hemisphere, I use a number of different approaches to the imaging part of a session.

- **A mindfulness pause.** Before asking a client to draw something, I create a mindfulness pause, taking time to allow images to emerge. By using a mindfulness approach, I slow the pace down and focus on the breath before talking through the coaching area of focus and inviting images to emerge in the client's mind's eye. Slowing the pace down helps the left hemisphere to relinquish the task, giving the right hemisphere the opportunity to take over.

- **Drawing in the moment.** However, the mindfulness pause doesn't work for everyone, as the mind can take time to settle and it can sometimes take a long time for the left hemisphere to relinquish control. In these circumstances I just ask clients to draw spontaneously, in the moment. The spontaneity of it, the no thinking about it, seems also to allow the right hemisphere to take over.
- **Working in the abstract.** Sometimes clients can become very judgemental of their creative abilities, which puts up a barrier to intuitive expression – is this possibly the left hemisphere annoyed at its lack of ability to perform the task? In these circumstances, I encourage people to just go with their instincts and intuition. This approach leads to abstract images that, in turn, lead to a deeper awareness. This may be because the client is creating images the left hemisphere does not recognise. It is not something it can relate to and it therefore disengages, allowing space for the right hemisphere to take over.
- **Playing.** I have also noticed that when encouraging clients to play with the materials, with no agenda, the resulting images can often be very powerful. The left hemisphere may have relinquished control because there is no logical purpose, allowing the right hemisphere to take over. The image seems to become unconsciously meaningful perhaps because it is a coaching session and the client may have already been reflecting on the focus for the session, so it is ready to emerge.

Bringing the hemispheres together

Throughout this chapter, I have been focusing on the importance of the right hemisphere. However, what gives us the ability to do things with what we experience, come to understand and know is the left hemisphere.

Through the image making process and the facilitated exploration clients can explore the whole of what is going on for them, connecting to the hidden and complex, giving them the space to talk about, experience and explore their images so they deepen their awareness, personal understanding and meaning, making insights. By doing this we also create a space that then enables the left hemisphere to do what it is good it at, but with the right information!

Once the client has real clarity and certainty about what the focus for them really is, the left hemisphere can then provide the analytical, logical and planning space, linking to what the client already knows, enabling them to move towards their coaching aims. Coaching with art can combine the strengths of both hemispheres.

Coaching with art example: bringing the hemispheres together

In the example used above in 'giving the silent right hemisphere a voice', the client, once he had identified through the language of art (right hemisphere) that the issue was values, was then able to reflect on how he wanted to work with this new insight, employing more left-hemisphere thinking. He was able to work on the real issue.

****

At the beginning of the chapter, I said I was looking for explanations for why coaching with art works so effectively. I wanted an explanation that I could share with my clients in my coaching practice, as well as fellow coaches, that would encourage them to be open to it. Understanding the connection between coaching with art and the right hemisphere has given me a rich seam of knowledge and information that has given both myself and my clients confidence in using this approach.

The functions of the right hemisphere add great value to our coaching. I have found that coaching with art gives the right hemisphere a voice, enabling our clients to access the non-verbal, unconscious parts of their internal world deeply and quickly. It enables them to externalise the complex, the paradoxical and the hidden. It gives them a safe space to explore emotional complexity and by so doing enables them to deepen their awareness and understanding, finding greater insights, new perspectives and greater personal meaning. It can, and often does, lead to shifts in awareness and understanding that lead to change. Coaching with art provides greater opportunities for aha! moments and transformational change.

There are, of course, other coaching approaches that access right-hemisphere functions, such as working with metaphor, body work and Gestalt approaches. However, I have found that coaching with art is particularly effective at this as it bypasses the need for detailed talking, questioning and analysis and just gets there.

As one participant on a workshop said: 'Normally I have to work quite hard to get through the analytic stage of unpicking [talking it through] . . . Making the image visible through art bypassed this, getting me straight to the issue without any disguise.'

Notes

1 McGilchrist, 2012, pp. 46–53.
2 McGilchrist, 2012, pp. 115–118.
3 McGilchrist, 2012, pp. 40–42, 79–83.
4 McGilchrist, 2012, pp. 79–83; Wikipedia, 2016.
5 McGilchrist, 2012, pp. 64–66.
6 McGilchrist, 2012, pp. 54–64.
7 McGilchrist, 2012, p. 76.

References

Edwards, Betty (2001). *The New Drawing on the Right Side of the Brain.* London: HarperCollins.
Gazzaniga, Michael S. (1998). 'The Split Brain Revisited'. *Scientific American*, July, pp. 51–55.
Gazzaniga, Michael S. and LeDoux, Joseph E. (1978). *The Integrated Mind.* New York: Plenum Press, pp. 148–149.

Gots, Jason (2012). 'Your Story Telling Brain'. *Bigthink*, 23 January. Retrieved from https://bigthink.com/overthinking-everything-with-jason-gots/your-storytelling-brain.

Malik, Kenan (2013). 'Divided Brain, Divided World?'. *Pandaemonium* blog, 21 February. Retrieved from https://kenanmalik.wordpress.com/2013/02/21/divided-brain-divided-world/.

McGilchrist, Iain (2012). *The Master and His Emissary: The Divided Brain and the Making of the Western World*. Princeton, NJ: Yale University Press.

Psychology Today (2016). 'Review of *Finding Flow* by Mihaly Csiakszentmihalyi', 9 June. Retrieved from www.psychologytoday.com/gb/articles/199707/finding-flow.

Schacter, Daniel L. (2002). *The Seven Sins of Memory: How the Mind Forgets and Remembers*. Boston, MA: Houghton and Mifflin.

Wikipedia (2016). Entry for 'Left-Brain Interpreter'. Retrieved from https://ipfs.io/ipfs/QmXoypizjW3WknFiJnKLwHCnL72vedxjQkDDP1mXWo6uco/wiki/Left_brain_interpreter.html.

Chapter 5

Art and coaching

> *'I have been struck by the progress [I have] achieved through the medium of art. I'm sure I have unravelled things much more quickly than might have otherwise been the case . . . I have found it incredibly powerful. I never cease to be amazed at what emerges apparently from nowhere.'*
>
> Sam, director of a professional organisation

I have talked about how art therapy and neuroscience have helped me shape my approach; however, I also wanted to know what was already happening in practice and how that could inform what I was doing. In addition to talking with coaches, I have also run a number of case study coaching programmes using art as the central approach. This has significantly helped me shape my approach as well as give supporting experiential evidence for working in this way. I have used these case studies, together with coaches' experiences in the workshops, throughout the book to demonstrate the approach and show what happens in practice.

I have spoken with coaches from different backgrounds, internal and independent coaches as well as new and experienced coaches to find out what already exists in practice. It was great to hear that coaches do use art and creative approaches; however, there seems to be no one particular approach, with each coach practising in a way that has evolved for them.

I also noted that art is used in a very broad sense, with some coaches taking their clients to art galleries, using the art as a starting point for a conversation, some using picture cards and others working with collage, dance, music or poetry. I have spoken to coaches with art backgrounds, some of whom use art in their practice and others who do not. I have also met art therapists who are trained coaches. There is a lot going on, but it doesn't seem very visible. This encouraged me to share my approach through workshops and CPD events. By doing this I have been surprised at how many coaches are really interested in using art and it has provided more insights that continue to help me shape my approach.

In this chapter I bring together art and coaching, exploring why coaching with art has an important place in our practice, by looking at

- next-generation coaching
- coaching in today's world
- the benefits of coaching with art, based on my own practice
- the applications of coaching with art, including a summary of the case studies I use in the book
- barriers to using art in coaching, in particular the barriers coaches put up
- the limitations to coaching with art

Next-generation coaching

In Chapter 1, I spoke about coaches referring to using art-based coaching as next-generation or second-generation coaching. As I said, it feels as though coaches are looking for something 'else' in their coaching practice – something that is deeper, more intuitive and transformational, perhaps wanting to move beyond models and processes which they may see as first-generation coaching.

As previously explained, this may be because one of the most rewarding outcomes in coaching is transformational shift, and my experience of coaching with art has shown this is an amazing and fast way to access a deeper, embodied level of self-awareness that can often create those shifts. Even if a shift doesn't occur, there always seems to be a greater sense of personal meaning and understanding that unlocks something for that person.

I also believe people are increasingly coming to coaching for that shift, for something that will give them lasting personal change, whether it is in their professional or personal lives. Using art has shown me that it does this powerfully and quietly, as long as the person being coached is open to the process.

Coaching in today's world

Coaching in todays' world brings with it many challenges. It is a world of instant gratification, where expectations are high and results are expected fast. It is a world where organisational clients need us to measure success and prove added value, whilst at the same time there is a downward pressure on fees and we are often expected to achieve a lot in a few sessions.

One of the very practical benefits of using art is that it can unlock core issues very quickly and often much faster than pure verbal coaching. As a result, I have been able to start working with my clients at a deeper and more transformational level earlier in the programme. As one person on a workshop said, 'it was a bit of a surprise how it got there so dramatically and quickly, tangibly and visibly'.

Another great benefit is that coaching programmes can be measured more consciously and tangibly. This is because the images created are 'keepable' and memorable, allowing us to look back over the coaching programme and clearly see the coaching outcomes and benefits from the sessions. This enables both coach and client to talk in a more tangible and detailed way about the success of the programme and added value. I know from experience that when doing this without art, it can be harder to gauge the extent of the progress as people often forget what it was like for them at the beginning and find it difficult to articulate what has changed for them. Words can also be forgotten, misremembered or exchanged for other words that may mean something slightly different.

Also, with our current working culture, the rise of the Internet and technology and future business demands, there is a need for innovative and creative solutions to business challenges. One of the benefits of coaching with art is it develops people's creative thinking and problem solving capabilities. It does this through its ability to hold complexity and paradox in one place, whilst accessing the more intuitive and global perspectives we have, as well as the peripheral. As one participant in a workshop said, 'It was a revelation that art is not about whether you can draw, it is about unleashing creativity and innovation'.

Benefits of using an art-based approach

In addition to these very practical benefits, they are also many client benefits. The previous chapters have highlighted those that cross over from art therapy into coaching and the benefits of working with the right hemisphere. Adding to these and reinforcing some others, I have listed below the most common benefits from my practice and, where appropriate, have included comments from my clients to demonstrate those benefits through their own experiences.

- Fast-tracking to the core of the area being worked on by unlocking hidden material

    'I still find it completely fascinating that these truths have emerged so quickly and profoundly, enabling me to articulate what have until now been nothing more than gut feelings' (Sam, director of a professional organisation).

- Holding complexity and paradoxes simultaneously that can be frustrating, emotional and unsettling, creating a safe place to talk about them and make sense of them

    'This reflection is quite paradoxical because my inner voice is in stark contrast to my general nature and love of adventure, my spontaneity and instinct, which I find have become supressed by the need to be . . . professional' (Keira, self-employed).
    'I can see a possible conflict between the love of India, with its wonderful bright, vibrant colours and palms trees, and the English landscape, with its birdsong and blue skies. . . I love both. Lots of contradictions' (Amelia, private client).

- Making breakthroughs

'I could never have imagined that the art would be such a powerful facilitator of thinking and lead to such rapid breakthroughs' (Sam, director of a professional organisation).

'I eventually pinpointed exactly which aspects of my research I want to write about. You could say my goal had changed and my understanding deepened through the art in coaching experience. This in itself was interesting and quite exhilarating' (Jaye, consultant).

'Both images seemed to be positioning me as a self-conscious individual who could focus something into controlled or uncontrolled beauty. In turn, this made me reflect that perhaps I should "work on myself" rather than "work on my writing" – a significant reflection given where the process arrived at the end' (James, executive coach).

- Supporting transformational change by helping a client get to a deeper level of self-awareness and understanding; the aha! moment

    'It was at that moment that I was struck by a thought that had an almost visceral impact on me. "I want to be with M by the sea". This felt incredibly strong and certain and really took me by surprise!' (Amelia, private client).

- Slowing down action-orientated clients, who just want to move on, and articulate clients, who can talk to deflect, defend and gloss over

    'There is no doubt that for me the image making was absolutely key to helping me over-ride my thinking brain and access my more knowing self' (Amelia, private client).

- Externalising those things clients find difficult to verbalise

    'I feel the awareness I need is already in my body, that I often know what I need before I can express it' (James, executive coach).

    'Sometimes I got a bit stuck ... But somehow instinctively ... I knew that I needed to define myself more before taking the outstretched hand!' (Amelia, private client, talking about the imagery she had created).

- Making sense of and resolving

    'I realise that I love my independence, but I need the stimulus of others ... Sole working brings out my inner voice quite strongly and sways between talking myself up and down (or out of things). This session has given me clarity around this' (Keira, self-employed).

- Spending more time with our client in areas of importance, giving them time to tune into their feelings and emotions and become aware of what is emerging for them

    As a coach I have noticed that, by staying with the image, it gives much more time to the inquiry and therefore we spend more time with areas of importance, not only within the image, but also through the image making process, and the exploration of themes across a number of images. For the client, they often experience flow, when they lose a sense of time. 'On occasions I forgot that Anna was in the room as I created images of what was happening in my world' (Jaye, consultant).

- Creating visual outputs that are memorable and 'keepable', enabling us to return to them to explore changes and understand emerging themes and patterns for our clients

    'my image was of blue sky, blue-and-green sea, wavy sand (interesting that this has been a theme in previous pictures), but previously the waves have represented scary things that I have needed to cross – water/snakes – but here the two figures are standing quite solidly on the wavy sand. . . Another light bulb moment: maybe the reason the water has been a recurring theme in my images is not because I am afraid of it, but because I want to be closer to it?' (Amelia, private client).

- Introducing fun and play, which can lead to creative thinking and deeper self-awareness and understanding

    'I have noticed myself becoming quicker to action in seizing the opportunity to be creative at work – identifying and using some new approaches; prioritising reflection more readily; giving myself permission to "own" the coaching space in creative as well as process driven ways' (James, executive coach).

    'The point is, the art in the coaching process encouraged me to experiment' (Jaye, consultant).

The applications of coaching with art

Coaching with art has many applications. It can be used in one-to-one coaching, group coaching and supervision (both one-to-one and group), as well as team coaching. It can be used in all forms of coaching, from executive through to life coaching and, within that, in all sorts of areas.

To demonstrate the wide application of art-based coaching, I have summarised below the case studies that are used in the book. Each one is different and includes executive coaching, business coaching, personal coaching, personal growth and development and unlocking 'stuckness'.

Please note that, although my clients have given me permission to use their experiences as case studies, their names and some of the context have been changed to maintain confidentiality and privacy.

Each case study gives an overview of the clients' experience of using art in their coaching rather than a session-by-session exploration of a coaching-with-art programme.

Case study 1: executive coaching

Sam had recently joined a professional organisation as a director to help effect change and bring in best practice. Having been there for seven months, Sam was finding the tensions between change and growth in the organisation frustrating and noticed how different her outlook was to others in the organisation. Sam and I contracted together to explore these tensions and how she could manage them to achieve her objectives. We agreed to have four 1.5-hour sessions, which took place over a five-month period. Sam created four images, one for each session.

The first two sessions were key for Sam in helping her to achieve her outcomes. The later sessions built on these two, with Sam starting to look towards the future.

In the first session, Sam explored the organisation and her role within it. Sam's initial image represented the organisation (Colour Image 1, plate section). When asking Sam where she was represented in the image of the organisation, Sam realised she wasn't in the image. After a while, Sam was able to include herself and added herself as the purple circle pushing into the larger green circle, which identified her feelings of difference and what Sam calls her 'otherness'. This has been a recurring theme for Sam throughout her career and became the focus for the next session.

In the second session, when Sam was creating her image, she was talking about a slinky toy. However, as we talked, Sam realised the image was in fact a curl, a powerful image of difference for Sam (Colour Image 2, plate section). Exploring this new-found meaning in her image, Sam talked about the feelings of difference as a child, which created a transformational shift for her – moving the feelings of difference in the organisation to one of an asset, rather than a burden. Sam was able to talk about her 'otherness' as something that 'provides an opportunity to see and do differently, so it can be a strength if I can tolerate being uncomfortable at times'. But it was the transformational shift that enabled Sam to let go of the negativity she was holding around her 'otherness' and really accept the value of what she was bringing to the organisation. 'I had a sudden realisation that my self-imposed, unacceptable otherness stems entirely from my very early childhood experiences... which are long behind me. I am sometimes still sad for the hurt-little-girl-me, but I recognise that I can safely let all of that go now!'

It was this breakthrough that enabled Sam to have the confidence at a much deeper level to manage the tensions in the organisation, whilst also nurturing herself and being open to future career plans that perhaps give greater outlet to who she is and her strengths.

Case study 2: business coaching

Keira came to me for a one-off two-hour coaching session and contracted with me to explore the direction she wanted to take her business as she was simultaneously feeling a sense of frustration and excitement with it.

During the session, Keira identified the conflict as being between what she wanted to do and what she felt she should be doing. 'My inner voice is in stark contrast to my general nature and love of adventure, my spontaneity and instinct, which I find have become supressed by the need to be . . . professional'.

Keira produced four images, of which two had the most meaning for her (Colour Images 5 and 6, plate section). These two images were drawn really quickly, one after the other, and were linked. One image reflected her inner voice (Colour Image 6, plate section) and the other was of something she called 'flow' (Colour Image 5, plate section). The inner-voice image was Kiera's inner critic that held her back from being in her 'flow' image. These two pictures and, in particular, the 'flow' image, created Keira's breakthrough point, as she said she 'suddenly felt free'.

Keira left the session being very clear about what she needed to do to take her business in the direction that she wanted. Keira gave herself permission to experiment more, focus on what her gut was telling her ('what I want to do') and not what she should do ('my inner voice'), giving herself space to check in with herself and her 'flow'. Keira took photographs of these two pictures and keeps them in a photo frame by her computer as a reminder.

Case study 3: personal coaching

Amelia is a private client and had, through changes in her relationships, reached a crossroads of opportunity and contracted with me to explore what for her was a meaningful life. Amelia wanted to get this new life right and have a sense of belonging. We contracted for four one-hour sessions, which took place over a period of seven months. Amelia created six images.

During the course of the programme, Amelia made a number of insights but by far the greatest was the need for maintaining a sense of self in a relationship. At the start of the programme Amelia had been very uncertain of what her life would be like, and created images with borders around them and with images of things she feared. Despite this, all of Amelia's images were hopeful and forward-looking. At the end of the programme, we looked back at all of Amelia's images, and whilst doing this Amelia focused on one that felt unfinished to her. Amelia then worked on it further until it became her closing image, summing up for her where she had got to; 'Anna and I talked about the image as a whole and I said that I felt it summed up what my life was becoming and how I wanted my life to be; random – no straight lines – go with the flow – free-flowing – no borders – off the page – full of colour, love and music. What a wonderful thing to aspire to. It feels really exciting and beautiful.' (This image is shown as Colour Image 4 in the plate section.)

Case study 4: personal and professional development

James contracted with me to explore his tension between productivity and creativity. This was forming part of his annual CPD and James wanted to make more time for creativity, which he felt was an essential part of who he was.

James and I contracted together to explore this binary issue, with a view to making more time for creativity in James's life and professional practice. We had four 1.5-hour sessions over a six-month period.

James created 11 images during the programme, and each session created a reflective insight for him and his approach to creativity, whether this was about his own writing or his professional practice. These were:

- session 1: 'perhaps I should "work on myself" rather than "work on my writing"'
- session 2: 'I was challenged to ask myself "do I believe in change? What am I risking if I spend time being creative?"'
- session 3: 'what I am learning overall is that it is internal and potential external judgement of the created piece and of me as a person which prevents me getting on the waterslide, and that it is the initial response that counts' ('the waterslide' refers to an image James created in this session; Colour Image 10, plate section).
- session 4: 'I notice as I look back that this image [the final image drawn in this session] has very strong similarities to elements of the earlier ones – it's almost as if its simplicity was waiting to emerge from the process'

Coming to the end of the programme, exploring all of his images, James then created his final three images (shown together in Colour Image 7, plate section). These were drawn very quickly, all at the same time. In these images, moving from left to right, James was able to see where he had been at the start, where he was now in the session and where he wanted to be. He was able to describe how these images made him feel – 'anxious' at the beginning, 'disconnected' right now and where he wants to be 'natural, peaceful and exciting'. He was also able to describe what, for him, a unified life where creativity and productivity are 'nested' together would be like, identifying clear measures of success to work towards. The 'nested' comes from his last image of where he wants to be (Colour Image 13, plate section).

James defined the three colours he used as yellow for his creativity, blue for his productivity and red for his ego and energy.

In his reflections after the programme, James said: 'The most significant result is far wider than the creativity/productivity debate: the final image of the nest, in which previously competing elements of my whole life are at rest together and support one another, will continue to speak powerfully to me as I develop as a person.'

Case study 5: unlocking 'stuckness'

Jaye is an HR professional who had recently completed a master's and wanted to build on her thesis and research to publish a book. Jaye had been putting off writing about her research and described herself as stuck. Jaye contracted with me to explore her blockages to writing, saying: 'I had been putting off writing about my research in any meaningful way'. Jaye's initial focus was on starting to write a book and exploring why she couldn't get started. Jaye's goal changed by the end of the programme.

We had four two-hour sessions over a period of seven months and Jaye created six images.

During the programme, Jaye moved from one session to the next, slowly coming out of her 'stuckness'. This is clearly shown by the difference between her first image (Colour Image 8, plate section), created in the first session, and her final image (Colour Image 9, plate section), created at the end of the programme.

The very first image shows Jaye's conflicting (my words) aspects to writing the book. The bottom-left is in watercolour and is Jaye's energy and ideas; the top-right was done in pastels and was the framework and more logical (my word) thinking around the book. The space in between is the blockage Jaye was experiencing in bringing the two together. This was later filled with a second drawing of the blockages. Jaye said she needed to know how to write a book and where to start.

In the final image, Jaye has again used watercolour and pastels and very similar colours to the first image. Here, they are all linked together. Jaye described the image as showing her energy and ideas, together with the possibilities and variety of ways that Jaye is now and could be writing about and communicating her research.

In Jaye's words: 'I did not achieve the goal of writing a book or even start to write the book. However ... the art-in-coaching process was completely successful in that I started to write articles about my research, understand the relevance of the research to my practice and longer-term goals. Most importantly, I eventually pinpointed exactly what aspects of the research I want to write about ... My goal changed and my understanding deepened through the art-in-coaching experience.'

In addition to the applications shown in the case studies above, the areas where coaching with art can be used are many, as long as the client is open to the process.

Coaching with art can be used for:

- transformational change
- personal growth
- emotional intelligence
- unlocking barriers to success, including unhelpful belief systems
- breaking through thinking loops
- breaking through behaviour patterns
- creative problem solving
- unlocking 'stuckness'
- resolving complex or paradoxical situations
- emotional complexity
- relational or systems complexity and tensions
- mindfulness and stress reduction
- confidence, self-worth and self-assurance

Coaching with art can then go on to be used to help our clients experiment and do something different, helping to push people out of their comfort zones in a safe space. It can do this through the created visual image as well as through inviting clients to try a different material, a different approach. For example, if a client always works with small pieces of paper and gets involved in the detail of their image making, you could suggest working with a large piece of paper and using materials that don't allow detail to be drawn.

Barriers to using art in coaching

So, with all the benefits described, not only in this chapter but also through art therapy and working with the right hemisphere, it may be a wonder that we aren't all using art as part of our coaching repertoire. This isn't the case. When talking and working with coaches, some quite powerful barriers have emerged that coaches can put up to working with art. Being aware of our own barriers is important for managing ourselves and holding the coaching-with-art space. It is also important for being aware of and exploring our clients' potential barriers.

The most powerful barriers people have are:

- limiting the use of art either through a perception of what it is for, or to stay in their comfort zones
- personal confidence
- perceptions of their own creativity, art and artists
- left-hemisphere bias

If you would like to work in this way, it is important you understand your own barriers to using art so you can hold them with curiosity and work on them. I did this for myself when starting to use this approach. Reflecting on my own barriers and building my confidence through practice and research has been essential for my personal growth and development around this approach. I encourage you to do the same.

Limiting the use of art

The first powerful barrier to working with art is limiting its approach. Coaches' perceptions of what this approach is, together with their own discomfort of it, often leads them to limiting what it can be used for. For example, one of the most common and most acceptable ways of using art seems to be when wanting a lighter touch to bring in a bit of fun or ice breaking when working with teams and groups.

Coaches seem to be most comfortable using art with other coaches and in supervision, recognising that coaches are very open to trying out something different for themselves. It is a safe space in which to use art.

This approach, because it is creative, can also be quickly boxed into an approach that is only for creative goals or for creative people. As one participant in a workshop said, clearly showing this perception: 'I am really looking forward to throwing some paint around but, of course, you couldn't use this in the boardroom.'

Art also seems to be more often used in personal coaching or with young adults and less often in executive or business coaching, with coaches concerned that in the latter spaces their professionalism may be called in to question.

What I have found particularly sad is having animated conversations about how transformational coaches have found a session when working with art, only to hear that it was one-off intervention, something a bit different that felt right just then and, despite the amazing outcome, it hasn't been used again.

Personal confidence

One of the main reasons coaches seem to limit the use of art in their practice is their confidence, which is often linked to their experience and knowledge of using it.

We all try things out and use them in the way they have been modelled for us either on courses, by other coaches or by our supervisors. Coaches who are artistic, or have art therapy backgrounds, may use art more regularly and in deeper ways. However, if coaches don't have this sort of background or haven't learnt how to work with image making, it can affect confidence in using this approach.

As mentioned above, coaches' confidence is also dependent on how they feel this approach would be received by their clients and, sometimes, the paying organisational client – and some fear it will be frowned upon and may not be seen as appropriate. Unlike many other approaches and techniques that coaches have no problem introducing to their clients, it seems that personal confidence is one of the most significant barriers stopping coaches from being able to introduce art-based coaching.

This lack of personal confidence comes through when coaches state that they couldn't work this way in, for example, a client's office, as they may be seen as 'playing' and the client may wonder why they are paying them to coach; however, my own experience tells me differently. I have used it, for example, with a leadership team, on more than one occasion, as part of their development to lead their organisation in the direction they want to go.

If you are starting to resonate with any of this, I invite you to hold your reflections with curiosity and just start to ask yourself why you might be feeling or thinking this way. Perhaps you can start to create or find an image that may reflect it for you.

Perceptions of our own creativity, art and artists

Underneath the barriers above lies the barrier of perception – the perception of our own creativity and that of art and artists – and I have come to realise that understanding these perceptions is important for unlocking our own barriers to using art.

When talking about working with art in coaching, people have an almost instinctive reaction to the word 'art'; it tends to polarise them. It is either seen as elitist, a rarefied world they have no place in, and may be accompanied by such phrases as 'I am not an artist', 'I am not creative'. At the other end of the spectrum it is seen as childish, something children do. It is playing and having an enjoyable time, 'which isn't what I do as an adult'. As I said in Chapter 1, art is either of great value, 'which is beyond my reach, or it is of very little value!

Even with the resurgence of interest in creativity, with such programmes as *The Great British Bake-Off* encouraging people to get creative in the kitchen, it is still seen as a hobby, a pastime, something to be done in leisure time, not in the work place.

And yet we know making art is instinctive and natural to us. Children readily create unabashed, great works of 'art', splashing paint around happily with no embarrassment at all! Why do we stop thinking of ourselves as creative? Where do our perceptions come from?

It would seem that as we grow and develop, we are guided through our education (formal and informal) as to what is important. Language and speech start to take centre stage along with more analytical and logical ways of being. We also learn to compare and judge ourselves against others and are influenced by the judgement of others.

However, talking generally with coaches, it has been really interesting to hear that our perceptions of our own creativity and art actually have a great deal to do with our experiences as children. Our perception of our own creativity and art is shaped by the views of our parents and how they talked about art and artists, together with what our teachers and other influential adults said about our creative endeavours. Most of us will recall a bad memory that may have spelled the end of our creativity. I have spoken to many people whose creativity was snuffed out by a teacher or other influential adult telling them they couldn't draw, or judging them as not having creative abilities. However, we also recall very happy memories of creativity. I remember sitting at the table getting paint and paper out and painting an elephant from memory, and building cardboard 3D games with my brother. You may remember getting involved in making something wonderful for a grandparent that is still, or was, treasured by them, or you may remember great joy spending hours colouring in.

Bad memories tend to come to fore and as such colour our confidence and perception of creativity. We put away our pens, paper, paint and pencils, fearing that we will fail or be ridiculed in some way, thinking we are not artistic.

Our own perceptions and pre-conceptions of 'art' will affect how we talk, think and use creativity in our lives and in our practice. You may already be judging the concept of coaching with art, questioning its relevance and credibility as a serious approach.

To be open to coaching with art, we need to reflect on our own art story and notice how this may be colouring our views and confidence.

> **What's your art story?**
>
> Take a moment to reflect on your own experiences of art and your art story.
>
> - What were you told about your own creativity? Was it supportive and encouraging or critical and dismissive?
> - What stories were you told about art and its place in the everyday world? Was it considered an important part of the world you were growing up in or was it sidelined?
> - How were artists and creative people perceived by those around you?
> - What is your own art history and story, and how has it shaped your perception of your own creativity?
> - How does this affect your approach to using art in coaching?
>
> I invite you to hold your responses with curiosity, to notice them and notice how they make you feel. Hold them whilst you read this book rather than letting them colour what you think is in the book.
>
> An image may have come up for you whilst reflecting. Why not capture that image, any way you want?

Left-hemisphere bias

Some of the reasoning behind the barriers we and our clients may put up to coaching with art may also come from left-hemisphere bias. The previous chapter looked at the different functions of the brain hemispheres and that the vocal left hemisphere is dominant most of the time. There is also cultural bias towards the left hemisphere that may also be at play.

Iain McGilchrist (2012) says that there is 'an entrenched prejudice that, whilst the right hemisphere may add a bit of colour to life, it is the left hemisphere that does all the serious business'. Given that coaching with art is linked to the right hemisphere, it may be that there are strong unconscious and cultural left-hemisphere biases that increase the possibility of coaches and clients diminishing and/or dismissing this approach.

When exploring the way we work and live, it is really noticeable that most of our educational system has been designed to cultivate the verbal, rational, logical left hemisphere, and the right hemisphere is virtually ignored. This bias is also born out in cultural behaviours and traditions, for example, seating important people to the right of the host (the right side is managed by the left hemisphere).

As we grow up, many of us leave our creativity behind as we learn to judge it and take notice of the judgement of others. We may often ignore our intuition and hunches (right hemisphere), mistrusting them because we can't explain and evidence them. Others may also ignore our intuition and knowing, again because we find it extremely hard to explain them to the satisfaction of our left-hemisphere world.

This left-hemisphere bias is also born out in the language we use. In our culture, we have phrases such as 'two left feet' and 'that was a left-handed compliment'. Remember, the left hand is managed by the right hemisphere. This bias can also be seen in the additional meaning for 'left-handed' across other cultures. For example, in Greek, *Skaios* also means ill-omened, awkward. In Hindi, *Ulta Haanth* also means opposite, wrong or bad hand, and in Swahili, *Kushoto* also means weak.

It is important to be mindful of this unconscious bias as it may be playing a part in why you and your clients could be putting up barriers to using this approach or limiting its use.

Hints, tips and some guidance on building confidence in your practice and getting started are covered in Chapter 9.

Limitations to coaching with art

There are many good reasons for coaching with art, but it does have some limitations. There are also boundary issues we need to consider, which are looked at in Chapter 7.

The most obvious limitation is that it is a physical process that requires coach and client to be present together. However, if you are using art in only one of your sessions it is very easy to refer to and to see the picture virtually if you continue with other sessions via Skype or using a similar method. If you work by phone, again the image can still be explored verbally in future sessions. Here it is helpful if both you and your client have a copy of the image and, as long as your client gives you permission, it is good practice to take a photo of all images created so that they can be easily referred to.

You may be wondering about the many art applications now available for tablets and PCs, where drawing and painting can be done with a stylus and shared virtually. These applications require both coach and client to be fully conversant with how these applications work and how to troubleshoot them. Also, the art making process as described in this book is very physical and this physicality is just as important as the image in how the approach works.

Coaching with art requires materials and for most of us these materials will need to be portable and easily used in the coaching space. It is quite easy to put together a portable pack of materials, and there is some advice and guidance on this in Chapter 9, but it does inevitably limit what you may be able to offer your client. For example, the size of paper may be smaller than perhaps your client might want to work with or you haven't been able to bring paints because the room you are using doesn't allow you to use those sorts of materials. This limitation may impact the richness of the outcome, but if your client really wants to work big and throw some paint around, you can always plan for it!

The space we work in is also important as we need to be mindful of how our client may feel about letting go and creating in, for example, a public space. This needs to be thought about carefully and it would be better to be able to have a private room or quiet space where clients can relax and just go for it, rather than thinking people are watching them. However, I do sometimes coach in public spaces and whilst I may not have the intention of running an art-based session, I will always carry with me a selection of felt-tip pens, colouring pencils, crayons and paper, just in case someone wants to do art and is feeling comfortable to do so.

Last, we need to recognise that for this approach to work, your client has to be open to it and what may emerge. This requires trust and rapport between you. If you don't have this or your client just isn't prepared to have a go, then you cannot force or hoodwink them into it. You will have to find another approach.

****

For me, art has a valuable place in my coaching practice, and I hope I have encouraged you to hold any perceptions you may have with curiosity and to explore further, stepping out of your comfort zone. One of our roles as coaches is to stretch our clients and take them out of their comfort zones. I believe we also need to do this for ourselves from time to time, so we are good role models for our clients.

I use art either as a central approach or alongside other approaches, as appropriate for the coaching client. Using art in coaching has provided amazing benefits for both myself and my clients, and is a wonderful way to work.

In the next chapters, I outline my approach and hope it gives you confidence in, as well as a foundation for, integrating art into your own coaching practice.

References

McGilchrist, Iain (2012). *The Master and His Emissary: The Divided Brain and the Making of the Western World*. Princeton, NJ: Yale University Press.

Silverstone, Liesl (1997). *Art Therapy the Person-Centred Way – Art and Development of the Person (2nd Edition)*. London: Jessica Kingsley.

Chapter 6

The principles of coaching with art

> 'The session worked for me at an unconscious and environmental level – a perfect storm – and has left me feeling good about the future.'
>
> Keira, self-employed

Through my research and experience, I have identified the core principles for my practice of coaching with art. These are the foundations for the next chapter, which details my approach (Chapter 7).

In this chapter, I bring together those principles as well as talk a bit about who can use this approach and supervision.

First, I want to summarise and remind the reader what art in coaching is about and what we mean by art in this context.

When talking about art in coaching, we are not talking about masterpieces, but rather any image that a client creates that has personal meaning for them. This image could be a drawing, a sculpture, a painting, a collage or a mixture. It is about self-expression, externalising through line, colour, texture and form an image of their interior selves.

There is a lovely quote from Tomoko Kawao, a *shodo* artist (Japanese calligraphy), which for me encapsulates this. Talking about her art in a TV programme, she said: 'What you feel in your heart flows through your arm and is expressed on paper. It's as if you can see your heart on the paper' (BBC4, 2017).

Through coaching with art, we deepen and enrich our coaching conversations with our clients, helping them move to a deeper level of awareness and understanding. It gives our clients access to the non-verbal, unconscious parts of their internal world deeply and quickly, enabling them to bring to the fore that which may be hidden but in need of recognition, and that which is just outside of awareness. It enables our clients to tap into their unconscious.

Once the client's image is externalised, the facilitated exploration with their coach provides the space for them to reflect on, and explore, their image with curiosity, taking as long as they need to find their own meaning and understanding within it. The client's connection to their image leads to shifts in perspective and thinking, which in turn lead to insights. These insights can then lead to personal growth and change, and can be transformational. Even if shifts don't occur, there is always a greater sense of personal meaning and understanding that unlocks something for that person.

Once the area to be explored using art has been agreed, coaching with art is achieved through the following five stages. These five stages reflect a coaching approach and have been adapted and extended from Leisl Silverstone's (1997) four stages in image work of person-centred art therapy. It is important to note that using art can be as much about finding the coaching area of focus for the client as it is about working with that area.

The following describe the five stages of coaching with art.

- **Stage 1. Imaging.** Creating the space to allow images to present themselves to our client's inner eye. Allowing images to emerge without judgement or censorship (right hemisphere) rather than illustrations of thoughts (left hemisphere).
- **Stage 2. Creating.** The client externalises their image and expresses themselves through making their art, trusting their intuition and instincts.
- **Stage 3. Connecting.** Working alongside our client to facilitate their understanding and meaning of their image; connecting them to their art in a client-centred way.
- **Stage 4. Coaching.** As the area of focus emerges and our client is clear about the area they want to work on, we move to coaching.
- **Stage 5. Continuing discoveries.** From session to session and outside the sessions, noticing and making space for ongoing emerging themes, understanding and insights.

Coaching with art works with the whole client, seeing them as healthy and as having all the resources and skills they need to achieve their desired outcomes. It is experiential, physical and creative with the image itself, providing a safe place for clients to express and hold the whole of what is going on for them.

Unlike words, which can be misremembered, reshaped or forgotten, the externalised image keeps. We can refer to it, know at once what it means and relate change to it. It is a safe, memorable and accurate way to share personal discoveries.

The core principles

The following core principles underpin my practice of coaching with art. Coaching with art:

- is client-centred
- creates a space for self-expression
- works with the whole
- is a physical process
- works with flow

- uses visual language
- always has a clear purpose and intent

Being client-centred

Being client-centred is central to coaching with art as it is only the person who is creating the art that knows what it may mean to them. The coach does not.

Being client-centred is taking a person-centred approach (as defined in the work of Carl Rogers; McLeod, 2007). This approach is non-directive and based on the belief that the person knows best, that the individual can reach their own potential when working in a climate of genuineness, acceptance and empathy. Person-centred coaching is integral to many coaches' practices and when coaching with art it is the central way of being. By being person-centred we are able to facilitate our client's exploration and connection to their image, holding up a mirror for our client, without interpreting, judging or guiding as it is they, not the coach, who know what the image means, even it takes time for that meaning to emerge.

The coach observes the art making process, they notice and facilitate, building a connection between the client and their image, with curiosity, without interpretation and without judgement. The purpose is to aid the client's exploration of their image and what is being evoked for them through their image, giving them the space and support to bring to awareness that which is truly going on for them.

By working this way, we are:

- working in the present moment – being fully present and inviting our clients to do the same
- enabling our clients to have confidence and trust in their intuition and instincts
- enabling our clients to work without censorship
- both – client and coach – working without judgement
- holding everything with curiosity
- observing and noticing, enabling the client to connect to their image

To be person-centred we need to create the right environment, and we can do this by meeting Carl Rogers' three basic conditions. Carl Rogers' said that when these conditions are in place, we create a climate where a client can, as he calls it, self-actualise and achieve their full potential. The three basic conditions are as follows.

- **Empathic understanding.** The coach deeply understands the client and is able to communicate that understanding to the client. We do this by giving our clients our fullest attention, being fully present for them in the coaching space. This creates a space for our clients to feel truly heard and therefore hear themselves. This, in turn, helps them trust themselves to explore further.

- **Providing unconditional positive regard.** The coach is accepting of the client as they are, believing that the client knows what is right for them. The coach has a non-judgemental attitude towards the client. When working this way, the client becomes more open to accepting themselves and thereby open to the possibilities of what they can become.
- **Congruence.** The coach is being genuine and authentic in the coaching space, bringing all of themselves into the coaching space. When the client experiences the coach as open and honest, they too may trust themselves to be the same, enabling themselves to shift and grow.

Through creating the person-centred environment the client will feel supported in the coaching-with-art space. This in turn will give them more confidence to step outside of their comfort zone, be open to the imaging process, trust and work with their intuition and feel more confident in making their art.

Creating space for self-expression

To coach with art, our clients need to feel they are in a space that enables them to relax and feel confident in externalising their interior images, in a way that feels appropriate for them, a space where they feel able to fully express themselves using their intuition and instincts, without censorship or judgement. It is only working in this way that their image will be a true reflection of what is going on for them at that time.

The coach creates this space through:

- the physical environment
- the contracting
- their own confidence
- the materials on offer
- how they hold and facilitate the process, building trust and rapport

The space then allows the client to externalise their interior world, including the complex, the paradoxical and the hidden. It gives them a safe space to explore emotional complexity, ambiguity and potential conflicts, and by so doing enables them to start exploring, reflecting and understanding what is going on for them, holding it with curiosity, taking the time they need for meaning to emerge.

Working with the whole

Coaching with art works with the whole, as it is, in all its complexity.

The image making process enables clients to make visible and tangible that which is going on for them internally. They can capture all of it within the image they create, even if it is hidden from them. This becomes a safer and easier space with which to explore their area of focus as it becomes something that can be seen.

Working with the whole enables the client to hold complex, paradoxical and conflicting thoughts, feelings, beliefs and experiences in one place. It provides a way of exploring those things that they may be finding difficult to articulate and allows those things that are hidden or just beyond their awareness to start to emerge.

When working with the whole we are initially accessing the right hemisphere, which perceives the world as whole, in relation to that which is around it and in context. We then, once the meanings have emerged and we have moved towards coaching, bring the left and right hemispheres together. The left hemisphere analyses and reasons, allowing the client to plan and take forward their insights and breakthroughs.

Working with a physical process

Coaching with art is a physical process. Our clients use their whole bodies when making their images and it is through this physicality that they convey their personal expression and their feelings associated with it. It is one of the reasons why coaching with art works at such a deeply emotional level.

The physical expression comes through how they approach their image making, including the energy they put into the marks and forms they make, how they stand or sit and the decision making process they have when choosing what to use and how to use it.

Working with flow

Clients often get the best outcomes when working with art if they work in 'flow'. Flow was first identified by positive psychologist Mihaly Csíkszentmihalyi (*Psychology Today*, 2016) as an experience that leads to greater consciousness and a higher level of achievement.

When experiencing flow, the client loses a sense of time; they become unaware of and are not interested in what is going on around them. They are fully absorbed and confident in what they are doing. It is a very enjoyable state where the task feels effortless and as though it is being directed by something other than yourself.

Flow comes, according to Csíkszentmihalyi, when the client is faced with a task that has a clear goal that requires specific and clear responses, and is a challenge that is just about manageable. When coaching with art we invite our clients to create imagery, which everyone is capable of doing, but which may often take them out of their comfort zone. If we are also creating the space of unconditional positive regard and trust, our clients are more likely to experience flow, immersing themselves into their imaging and externalising of their image.

Using the language of the image

Coaching with art uses the language of the image, the language of art. We may, for example, talk about the colours used, the textures and marks made and the media used, such as crayons, paint or modelling clay, or we may talk about the imagery itself.

Using visual language is one of the keys to unlocking the hidden and deepening awareness. This is because it takes the pressure off the client having to explain everything, and can also stop clients from becoming overly analytical. As a result, clients stay in the space longer. It is also a safe and uncomplicated language that allows clients to tune into their feelings and emotions and deepen their awareness and understanding, without feeling that they have to label everything. They can just hold 'knowing' it and 'being' with it.

Having clear purpose and intent

Coaching with art may raise areas for a client that fall outside of coaching and/or a coach's abilities and it is important that both the coach and client know what happens in these circumstances. This should be included as part of the boundaries and ethics of the contracting.

Coaching with art works at a deep level and can often unlock the hidden. If art-based exercises are too broad or have no real coaching intent behind them, there is a risk that the client may start to make visible experiences and memories that have stayed hidden for a long time. These may be experiences and memories that the client is not ready to recognise or does not wish to know, and may not be part of the coaching contract. There is also a risk that the coach could stray into areas they are not qualified for or do not have the abilities to support.

To manage these boundaries, it is therefore really important that coaching-with-art exercises are introduced with a clear coaching purpose and intent. This purpose and intent is set as part of the contracting for a client's programme, as well as the areas of focus that may emerge for the client in each session.

The coach

The coach does not have to consider themselves an artist to coach with art, but what they do need is to feel confident in themselves as a creative person as well as confidence in the approach. They will also need to be very familiar with the materials they bring to a coaching session, understanding how they work and what a client could potentially do with them. This is important as the coach not only facilitates the process but also needs to be able to demonstrate how to use the materials they offer. This in turn gives confidence to the client, who may not have worked with art before, or for a long time. The coach needs to be aware that there is often an unconscious expectation from the client that the coach will be the 'expert' in the materials. (Materials are covered in Chapter 8 and hints and tips for getting to know your materials are provided in Chapter 9.)

A coaching-with-art coach is also usually an experienced coach; however, it is the confidence in the approach that actually matters. I have worked with newly qualified coaches who have embraced this approach wholeheartedly, and very experienced coaches who have shied away from it. If this approach resonates with you and your practice, then it will be right for you.

The client

Anyone can be a coaching-with-art client. They do not have to be able to draw or consider themselves creative, they just have to be open to the process and allow themselves to be taken a little out of their comfort zone.

Supervision

Supervision and creating a safe space to reflect on your practice is important for all coaching. It is particularly important when working with art and its ability to work with the unconscious. Supervision helps us to manage our boundaries and ethics as well as our personal resourcing and patterns when working this way.

References

Psychology Today (2016). 'Review of *Finding Flow* by Mihaly Csiakszentmihalyi', 9 June. Retrieved from www.psychologytoday.com/gb/articles/199707/finding-flow.
McLeod, Saul (2007). 'Carl Rogers'. *Simply Psychology*. Retrieved from www.simply psychology.org/carl-rogers.html.
BBC4 (2017). 'The Way of Shodo: Artist Tomoko Kawao'. *The Art of Japanese Life*. First aired June 2017. Available at www.bbc.co.uk/programmes/p056qcjq.
Silverstone, Liesl (1997). *Art Therapy the Person-Centred Way – Art and Development of the Person (2nd Edition)*. London: Jessica Kingsley.

Chapter 7

Coaching with art in practice

> *'I didn't feel I could be artistic and it was a revelation how much I got from just a few scribbles – understanding the power of just putting something down on paper and not thinking in words.'*
>
> *Rosemary, workshop participant*

When coaching with art we can consider it as either our main coaching approach, one where art is central to each session, or one where we use it as one of a variety of approaches that we introduce as and when we feel it would be beneficial. The choice is ours and depends on how it fits with our coaching practice.

Whether we want to build an art-based practice or we want to have it as part of a wider repertoire, the approach to working with art is very much the same. The differences may come in the contracting and then how we build on an art-based session within the wider programme with our client.

In this chapter, I outline my practice to coaching with art and the areas we need to consider when working this way – whether it is your central approach or as part of a repertoire of approaches. I have included examples from the coaching case studies, where appropriate, to help demonstrate coaching with art in practice. All the case studies in the book are from coaching programmes where art has been the central approach used.

Many of our usual coaching practices apply when coaching with art. However, there are some practices we need to adapt to meet the requirements of coaching with art, and new ones we need to know about when practising with art. These practices are covered through looking at:

I. contracting for coaching with art
II. preparing for coaching with art; preparing for a session
III. the first session
IV. overcoming clients' potential barriers
V. which exercise?
VI. facilitating the process for our clients – the five stages to coaching with art:

Coaching with art in practice 65

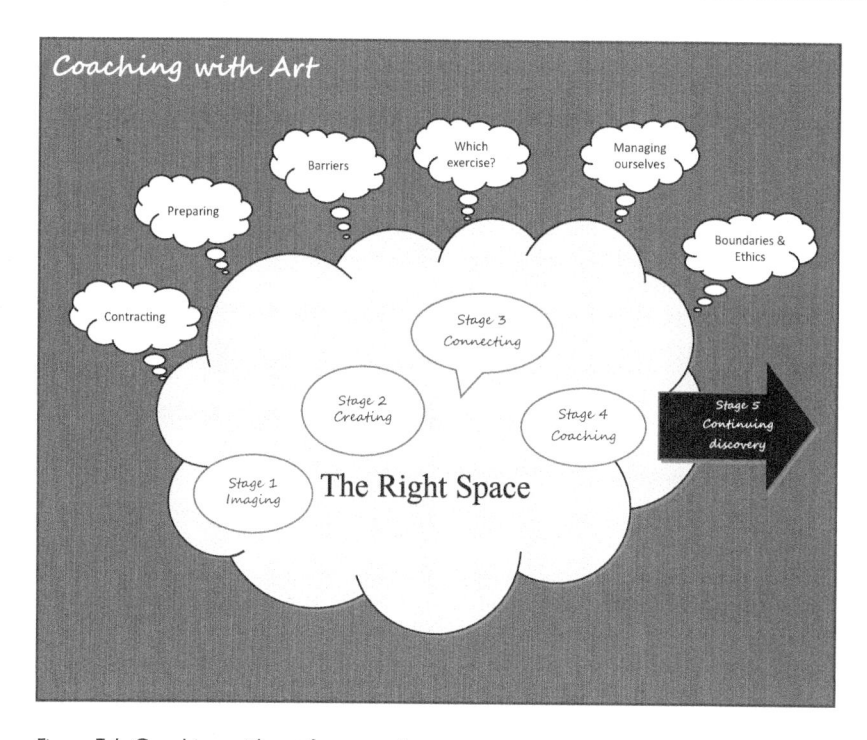

Figure 7.1 Coaching-with-art framework

       stage 1: imaging
       stage 2: creating
       stage 3: connecting
       stage 4: coaching
       stage 5: continuing discoveries

VII. managing ourselves in the process
VIII. boundaries and ethics
IX. the final session and closing out

I Contracting for coaching with art

As with all coaching, we start with a chemistry call or meeting and contracting. Contracting for the programme tends to happen over the course of the initial discussions and within the first session. Re-contracting may also occur as coaching goals evolve and change as the coaching progresses and contracting for each session happens as part of that session.

Contracting for coaching with art is the same as all coaching, with some added areas we need to consider.

- **Explain your approach.** Explain why you use coaching with art and how it supports your client in achieving their coaching goals.

  For me, an important aspect to my contracting was stating that my clients' coaching goals came first. If at any time I felt it was more appropriate to use a different approach, or the client wanted to stop, then it was okay to raise this in the session and agree to work differently.
- **Define what is meant by 'art'.** It is important for clients to be clear about what is meant by art in coaching as it helps to manage expectations and any potential barriers. It is important for them to know anyone can work this way and that it is not about being able to draw or create masterpieces; it is about self-expression.
- **Raise awareness of how deeply this works.** This approach can work at a deep level and your clients can unlock hidden aspects of themselves. Clients should understand the emotional depth of this approach so they can decide if they wish to take part.
- **Be clear about the focus of a session.** Following on from the above, explain that this approach is introduced with a clear coaching purpose and focus, and it has clear boundaries.
- **Clarify your ethics and boundaries.** All coaching has ethics and boundaries included within its contracting. For coaching with art and its ability to work deeply and with the hidden, it is important for clients to know the ethics and boundaries you work within. There may be areas that come up for a client that fall outside of coaching and/or a coach's abilities. It is important that both you and your client know what happens in these circumstances. (See also section VIII in this chapter.)
- **It is okay to stop.** Re-assure your clients that they don't have to openly explore their image with the coach if they don't want to, and that they can stop at any time if it starts to feel too challenging or uncomfortable.
- **Explain how you run a session.** Explain how you run a coaching-with-art session, including what is expected of your client and your role in running the session. (See also section VI in this chapter.)
- **Agree the coaching space.** Agreeing the coaching space you will be working in together is important for clients to feel safe and at ease when working with art, so they don't feel overlooked whilst creating. For example, when contracting with Jaye, we contracted for three sessions to be in the studio and then for the last session to be at her home. During the programme this changed, and Jaye re-contracted for the last session to be in the studio, as the space felt right for her.
- **Agree the length of time.** Agree the duration of sessions and ensure there is enough time to enable your clients to create their images, for you to facilitate

their exploration and then work together on what emerges. The number of sessions you agree is, as with all coaching, dependent on the work you are contracting to do together. For example, with the case study programmes in this book, clients' sessions varied from one to two hours depending on their needs and preferences. Most then had four sessions, except for Keira, who contracted for a one-off two-hour session. Also, the length of the coaching programmes varied and was anything from five to seven months.

- **Agree on what happens to clients' images**. All the images created belong to your client and what happens to their images at the end of each session should be agreed. These images are private and confidential and should not be shared with anyone without your clients' permission. If you are holding clients' images on their behalf, it is important they know they are kept in a safe and confidential place. If clients take images away, you should include contracting for permission to take photos, explaining that it enables their images to be available for each session if your client forgets to bring them with them. Digital copies should be held in a secure and confidential place.

  If clients take their images away, it is important to contract for your client to bring previous images to future sessions so they can be available to refer to if needed. It is also important to ensure your client brings all images back to the final session as they form an integral part of the final session and review of their programme. (See also section IX in this chapter.) For example, as part of the contracting for the case studies, we talked about the images and I asked permission to take photographs. However, I actually did this at the end of each session, as it felt right not assume it was okay based on a previous permission. Images created are deeply personal and clients can feel differently after each one is created.

- **Ensure confidentiality**. As with all coaching, coaching with art is a private and confidential space. When contracting it is important that this explicitly includes the space where we ask our clients to externalise their visual images and the holding of images, both physically and digitally. Images should not be shared with anyone on any platform without the express permission of the person who has created them.

When contracting for using art in a coaching programme, what you contract for will depend on whether you are using art as the central approach to the programme, or whether it is one of a number of approaches you may introduce. If it is the former, it is important your clients are fully aware of this when deciding to work with you, and your contracting needs to include an explanation of your approach and how it works, together with boundary and ethical principles. If your approach is to use art as one of a number of possible approaches, you may want to mention this in your initial contracting so you can manage any potential barriers at an early stage. Then, when you choose to introduce art, you need to take some time to contract for it as part of that session.

II Preparing for coaching with art

Preparation is key to successful coaching and when coaching with art there are a number of additional things we need to think about when preparing for an art-based coaching session. These include:

- creating the right space
- managing the time
- the materials you are offering

You also need to consider if there is enough rapport and trust to bring in art-based coaching if it is new for this client.

Creating the right space

Above, I mentioned that it is important to work in a space where the client feels safe and at ease when working with art. For many, working in this way takes them out of their comfort zone and can be quite challenging. It is important that the space you work in gives them a feeling of safety and not of being exposed to potential onlookers who they may perceive as judging them. A question you could ask yourself is: 'would I be happy to create my own images in this space?'

When choosing a space to work, we also need to consider whether it is fit for purpose. Consider the following questions.

- How am I proposing to work with my client?
- Is there enough space to do this?
- Is there a table for my client to work on?
- Would they prefer to work on the floor and, if so, could they?
- Does the venue restrict the use of any materials? Some venues may not be happy with paints, for example.
- Do the floor or table need protecting in any way? For example, the dust from using pastels and charcoals can become deeply embedded in carpet.
- What facilities do we need? For example, will your client need to wash their hands frequently?

The space I use most of the time is my studio, which means my clients can work in any way that feels right for them. However, you don't need to use a studio. When having my own coaching sessions, my coach hires a room and has plastic on the floor underneath the table. I also use plastic sheeting in the rooms I use for the workshops. However, when running CPD events I often have no idea of the room, so I err on the side of caution and take a selection of materials that can be used anywhere. These include manageable paper sizes, wax crayons, colouring pencils and felt-tip pens.

Managing the time

As part of the contracting conversation you will have agreed the length of time for sessions to ensure there is enough time to coach with art. Sessions should be managed in a way that gives enough time for:

- you to run the imaging process
- your clients to create their images and not feel rushed into finishing
- you to facilitate their full exploration so your client can connect with their image, allowing their meaning to emerge
- you both to work together on what emerges

The above are fully covered in the five steps to facilitating the process for our clients in section VI of this chapter.

Sometimes it feels absolutely right to do an imaging exercise and it happens right at the end of the session. If this happens, it is really important you agree with your client exactly what there is time for and whether to continue or defer to the next session. This may mean setting a time limit in which your client can create their image, and only exploring at a high level. Check this is okay.

If you are working with groups, it is vital the session length enables everyone to have the time they need to create and explore their images. People shouldn't be missed out or have less time due to time issues. As part of the contracting for group sessions you may want to agree an allocated amount of time per person.

Time management around using art is important if clients are to maximise its potential. Having a feel for how long the process of coaching with art takes comes with practice and experiencing it for yourself.

The materials you are offering

The materials your client chooses as part of their image making exercise are as important as the image itself. The choices they make are integral to their self-expression. Therefore, being able to offer a good choice of mediums (pens, pencils, paints, collage, clay etc.) and supports (paper, card etc. on which we create art) is important.

As part of your preparation, spend some time thinking through the materials you would like to offer your client. You may want to consider the following.

- **Client preference.** When contracting and discussing this approach your client may have expressed a preference for working in a particular way. Can you accommodate this?
- **Your preference.** You may have already indicated the choice of materials you offer as part of your introductory conversations and you need to ensure you have those with you.

- **Portability**. If you are working in a dedicated space the choice of materials on offer can be wide; however, you may have to move around to where clients are based. Therefore, you will need to think about portability. You may be hiring a space, working in a meeting room at a client's premises, or in an open space. In these circumstances you need to think about what materials you can carry, how easily the client can use them in the space and how you are going to transport them. Chapter 9 includes some guidance on putting together a portable pack.
- **Knowing your materials**. Part of your role as coach is to be able to demonstrate and advise your clients on the materials you offer. As previously mentioned, there is no requirement to be an artist or to draw; however, it is important that as part of your preparation you become familiar and confident with the materials you offer and know how to use them. I encourage you to explore, experiment and play. This will enable you to see how it feels to use them, how far you can stretch them in making visual imagery, and their limitations. It will also increase your own creativity – and you never know where that may lead you!

    Having an understanding of the materials is very helpful for my clients. For example, James was trying to merge the colours in one of his images and because, through observing his process, I knew he was using water-based colours, I could suggest using water. James said that 'this transformed it into something living for me, with the colours blended.' Clients do have an unconscious expectation that the coach will have 'expert' knowledge of the properties and uses of the materials provided. (Materials are covered in Chapter 8 and in Chapter 9 I include hints and tips around getting to know materials and their uses.)
- **Use of materials to explore coaching aims**. By understanding the variety of mediums and supports available (don't forget sculpture and collage) you will also be able to see how they could be used when working on particular issues with your clients. For example, if someone wants to loosen up and be free you may want to encourage them to work with large pieces of paper with large graphite sticks, charcoal or paint. Alternatively, if someone wants to let go of detail, you may only want to offer soft pastels that can't make detailed marks. Only by exploring the choice of materials available can you start to understand the possibilities of the different ways to create visual imagery and how you can use them in your coaching practice.
- **Accessories**. Don't forget the accessories – things like glue, pencil sharpeners, scissors and sticky tape.

Please **don't** use flipchart markers, flipchart pads and whiteboard markers as part of your materials kit. These have very particular adult associations with work and with the left hemisphere (analytical, logical, reasoning). When working with art we want people to tap into their inner child of play, creating images instinctively without censorship or judgement.

III The first session

I have included the first session separately, as this is the session where your client is introduced to the coaching-with-art space. It is important that the first session enables them to start to feel comfortable within the space.

At the start of a coaching-with-art programme, the elephant in the room for the client is always the materials and the knowledge that at some point their coach is going to ask them to do some art. This can be a significant barrier and starting the first session by demonstrating the materials, showing the client where everything is and then encouraging them to play with everything helps to overcome this. When doing this, there is no agenda.

When I demonstrate, I take the biggest piece of paper on offer and make a mess over it, talking through how each medium works and how they work together or not! I have discovered that it is best to have materials that look used. Anything new is taken out of its packet, crayons are snapped in half and paints are left looking a little bit messy. This makes everything accessible and gives people an unconscious permission to use them.

When encouraging clients to play I am sometimes in the room and sometimes not, depending on whether I am getting refreshments. The most important thing is to give them as much time as they need to familiarise themselves with the materials so they start to relax into mark making, collage or whatever else they are drawn to. Questions can be answered and materials re-demonstrated as needed.

Although these play sessions have no agenda to them, they can sometimes lead to coaching conversations and deeply meaningful images. (More of this later in section V, which explores the different exercises we can use, including play.)

The first session is also where you may come up against your client's barriers to working with art. Although you may have started to explore this as part of your contracting together, clients can be taken by surprise by how strong their barriers may be. You may need more time to explore this in your first session and may also need to be more flexible in your approach.

IV Overcoming clients' potential barriers

> The range of media and lack of constraints to approach are both freeing and somewhat intimidating (at first), but a "just-go-with-it" approach helped [me] to move beyond this quite quickly.
>
> Sam, director of a professional organisation

I am sure we have all experienced times when clients have put up barriers to new techniques that involve creativity, whether in a one-to-one, group or team setting – mutterings of 'I can't draw', 'I'm not visual', 'I'm not creative'. A mixture of embarrassment and perhaps fear of looking silly. Some stubbornly ignoring the exercise and writing words!

Take a moment to think back to your own art experiences and story. What barriers were there for you? It is likely that your client's art story is working as a barrier for them too.

Coaching with art does take people outside of their comfort zone, but it shouldn't be to such an extent that it stops them from being able to create meaningful visual imagery. If your client is finding this too much of a stretch, there are some things you can do to help.

- Ask them about their art story and encourage them to explore their potential barriers.
- Remind them that the exercise is about visual language and not about creating a work of art. There is no requirement to be artistic or creative.
- Share with them some example images that demonstrate the sorts of things that other people have created. Please note these images should only be shown if you have permission to do so. I have a number of images on my website's 'Gallery' page you can use as well as the images in this book. All these images have had permission from their makers to share them.
- Explain, in a left-hemisphere way, the purpose of the exercise and the benefits to them and their coaching aims for working in this way. Explain the left and right hemisphere's ways of working as outlined in Chapter 4 and the benefits of working more with the right hemisphere.
- Invite them to play with the materials, doodle with no real purpose and see what emerges (see the free exercise in section V).
- Try using existing images such as pictures in a magazine or found objects in the space in which you are working as a starting place for exploration. Consider collecting a selection of postcards to use.
- Suggest working with collage using images cut or torn from magazines as an easy first step to externalising their visual images. When working this way my clients sometimes go on to embellish their images with marks using other materials.

It is really important for a client to be open to the process and go with their intuition when working with art. This means there needs to be strong trust and good rapport with their coach. If none of the above helps and a client really doesn't want to work in this way, find another approach. Come back to coaching with art another time if it feels right and the client has reached a place where they want to give it a try.

V Which exercise?

The most frequently asked question by coaches is 'how do you know what exercise to use and when do you introduce it?'

The starting point is knowing when to introduce an exercise, as when you know this you will almost always know what exercise would be appropriate. However, as part of contracting for a session, I also invite my clients to create at any time if they feel they want to and not just to wait for me to introduce an art-based exercise.

When to introduce an art-based exercise

Knowing when to introduce an art-based exercise is similar to knowing what area you work on with your client in your usual practice. It is about being fully present with your client and alert to what draws their energy and attention. This becomes your client's emerging area of focus and could be the area on which you would base your exercise. Bear in mind that it is important for your client to agree what they want to explore using art, otherwise it becomes your agenda.

Sometimes the client lets you know when to introduce an exercise as in that moment they know what they want to focus on, letting you know they would like to use art to do this.

You could also ask your client during your coaching conversation if something has come up for them that they would like to explore using art.

If you become unsure about introducing an exercise, ask your client if they would like to explore the area you are thinking of and see how they respond. They may agree, or the question may spark off a different and more meaningful area for them.

Whatever exercise you do, it should have a clear coaching purpose and you should know why you are introducing it. If you don't, you may end up incorporating general open questions about your client where the boundaries are so wide you may inadvertently stray into areas beyond coaching. For example, a question such as 'what comes up for you today?' is very broad and personal. It could take your client anywhere. Instead, your art-based exercise should be coaching-focused and asked in the context of the coaching aims. For example, if you have been engaged to work with someone on their confidence in meetings, this question could be rephrased as 'reflecting on the meetings you have had since we last met, and your confidence, what comes up for you today?'

Which exercise to use?

Once you have identified the area of focus for an art-based exercise and have agreed this with your client, you are ready to introduce it. What shape this exercise takes will usually come to you in the moment as the exercise that best fits with the area your client's attention has settled on.

Art-based exercises fall into the following types:

- a guided exercise exploring a particular scenario
- an imaging exercise focused on a word or phrase that has emerged as important for the client
- a guided metaphor-based exercise

- an in-the-moment, 'just-draw-it' exercise
- a free exercise or playing!

For the first three types of exercise I often use a 'mindfulness imaging' process where I create a pause that slows the pace down, allowing the left hemisphere to relinquish control of the task and the right hemisphere to take over. (I explain this more fully in section VI.)

Sometimes I don't have to introduce an exercise, as the client asks to create something. An area has emerged for them that they feel strongly they want to explore using art. They work unguided, in the moment, with their intuition.

A guided exercise: exploring a particular scenario

A guided exercise is guiding someone through a particular scenario that is relevant to the coaching aims, or relates to what the client has been exploring. We create a space through the imaging process that allows an image to emerge to our client's inner eye that they then externalise and make visible using the materials in the space provided.

For example, in our third session James recounted an experience he had whilst out walking with his wife and how, when they stopped at a pub, he started to write. This was a shift for James as he would normally have felt rude writing in the company of others. We agreed to do an art-based exercise around this scenario to see what came up for him. I started the exercise with a mindful pause, inviting James to close his eyes and become fully present. Then, staying in the mindfulness space, I guided James through his walk, arriving at the pub and writing – recounting what he had told me. I then asked James how he felt being in that creative space, inviting him to hold those feelings before asking him to allow an image to emerge. There are plenty of pauses in this process, giving time for James to experience the guided exercise and allow images and feelings to come to the fore. I then finished by asking James, when he was ready, to gently open his eyes and capture his image any way he chose using the materials in the room (Colour Image 10, plate section).

Exploring this image and asking what would enable James to hold a creative space, James talked about the red arcs. These were waterslides, and once you get on you will be carried to the centre. James further reflected that it was both his internal judgements and potential external judgements of him as a creative person that prevented him from getting on the waterslide and taking him to his creative space.

A guided exercise example: going for an interview

This example gives you an indication of the approach I take when using mindful imaging. You could use this example as a basis for creating your own.

'Close your eyes, relax and push away your thoughts... [Pause] You are entering a building where you are going for your interview... You are in

> reception – you see a notice: 'Interviews this way'. You follow the arrow, along a corridor. You come to a door marked 'Interview Waiting Room'. You go in. The room is empty, except for chairs along a wall. There is a door with a notice: 'Interview; wait here please'. You sit down, and as you sit, waiting, you go back in time to other interviews you have gone for. . . [Pause] Spanning down the years, perhaps to your first interview. . . [Pause] What are you noticing? [Pause] What is being said to you? [Pause] How are you feeling? What is coming up for you? [Pause] And you remember how you felt. . . [lengthy pause] And now you cross over to the other side of the room and sit on a chair facing the one you just left – you get in touch with yourself now – your adult self – and you reflect on the belief you hold about yourself now, to do with interviews. . . [Pause] And when you are ready, open your eyes and convey your experience on paper, however you want.'
>
> The pauses should be long enough to enable your client to feel themselves into their inner space and experience being there.

An imaging exercise based on a word or phrase

In this exercise, rather than being a scenario, it is a word or a phrase that is the basis of the exercise. For example, in James' first session where we started to explore James' tension between creativity and productivity, the feelings around his creative self started to emerge. At this point we agreed to do a mindful imaging exercise where I asked James to allow an image to emerge of 'him the writer, him the poet'. Another example comes from Sam's second session that resulted in her image of a curl (Colour Image 2, plate section). Here, the imaging focused on the word 'otherness'.

The word 'success' is a common one in coaching as we often ask our clients what success would look like for them. They can often find this hard to describe and it would make a great art-based exercise.

A guided exercise – using metaphor

A guided exercise based on a more metaphorical scenario could be introduced if it feels appropriate to the coaching topic you are working on together. For example, when Sam came into her third session she was very tired and under a lot of pressure. Sam started talking about feeling guilty when doings things just for herself. Sam was noticing she was always doing and not just being, even though she really enjoyed just being. We agreed this was the area of focus for the session and I introduced a guided exercise using metaphor. I started with a mindfulness pause, spending time bringing Sam in to the present moment. I then asked Sam to visualise a box containing all those things that made up 'Sam'. After a long pause, to enable Sam to image her box, I asked Sam to rummage around in the box and see what was there. Sam did this in silence. After another long pause, I invited Sam to capture her image in any way she wanted using the materials in the room. The resulting image (Colour Image 11, plate section) was the starting point for a coaching conversation exploring what Sam wasn't making time for that was important to her.

You could expand any visual metaphors you use in your coaching into an art-based exercise. For example, when exploring the dynamics in a professional relationship this metaphor is often used: 'If you and X (X being the other party in the professional relationship) were going to a fancy-dress party, what would you both go as?' Rather than talking about the image, think how much richer the conversation may be if it was the basis of an art-based exercise?

In-the-moment, 'just-draw-it!' exercise

This exercise is good for when

- someone is struggling with the mindfulness imaging approach and is either not able to allow images to emerge or is starting to judge themselves and what they are drawing
- it feels like the right thing to do in that moment, and the energy from your client enables you to say 'just draw it'; this is usually followed by very intuitive in-the-moment drawing based on what they are feeling
- someone is finding it hard to articulate what they are experiencing; here, asking them to just draw what they are experiencing in any way they want to, inviting them to go with their intuition, can break through and help them find the words

There is no mindfulness imaging process for these exercises, as they are in the moment. These exercises encourage your client to go with whatever feels appropriate for them, without censorship and judgment – to trust in their intuition. The spontaneity of the approach seems to allow the right hemisphere to take control and allow deeper awareness and meaning to emerge.

A good example of this is Keira's 'flow' picture (Colour Image 5, plate section). In Keira's session, to help her move away from judging herself and from wanting to create good images to take home, I asked her to draw in the moment. This allowed her to break free of her thinking left hemisphere and draw intuitively in the moment.

A free exercise or play!

This is when we ask our client just to draw without imaging beforehand; no guidance, just draw and see what comes up. It is about giving your client permission to play and the confidence to trust their instincts and intuition, permission to pick up whatever medium they want to use, whatever colours they want to use, create any mark, shape and so forth. It is very similar to the 'in-the-moment' exercise and is particularly good for clients who don't appear to be making progress, are talking too much, going round in circles or doing a lot of deflecting. This exercise can get underneath the surface of lots of left-hemisphere processing. It is also useful for when a client comes in with no idea about what they want to use their coaching session for!

Please note that this exercise should be set up in the context of the coaching programme so it has clear purpose and intent, otherwise it could take your client anywhere.

A good way to start this exercise is by generally exploring what is coming up for them, in the context of the contracted-for programme, and then after a little exploration ask them to start drawing in that moment, inviting them to play with the materials, and just see what emerges for them. By starting this way, the exploration becomes about the coaching aims and is not left open.

Interestingly, in the initial sessions with clients, when inviting them to play with the materials as part of introducing them to the coaching space, this play can also lead to images that form the starting point for coaching conversations.

For both Sam and Amelia, their play pictures started to emerge into images that formed the basis of our coaching conversations. Sam's play picture became an image of the tensions between change and the status quo in the organisation she joined (Colour Image 1, plate section). This is discussed in more detail in Chapter 4, where it is used an example to explore working with the whole. As Sam and I started exploring this image, Sam added to and changed it to include herself in the organisation, which led to her revelation that she still felt an outsider in her job.

When Amelia started to play with the materials in her first session, she talked whilst creating and this process started to lead to insights for her (Colour Image 12, plate section). This moved naturally into a coaching conversation with Amelia adding to her 'play' picture. Further explorations of the image enabled Amelia to talk about being at a life crossroads, wanting to make a meaningful life and how concerned she was at being drawn into her old life – all relevant to her coaching programme.

Other exercises

There are many opportunities to turn our usual coaching approaches and questions into art-based exercises. For example:

- the Miracle Question – this could easily be used as the basis of an imaging exercise
- an exercise based on an event such as New Year – great for imaging around the future
- how about a metaphor-based exercise around a package arriving, or opening an attachment to an email, that is delivering something your client needs or wants but just can't articulate: what image emerges for them?

- think about some of the questions we use; could they be used for an art-based exercise? For example, the question 'what's stopping you?' could easily form the basis of an imaging exercise

The opportunities are endless.

Take a moment to notice what you use in your usual practice, and ask yourself if it could be the basis of an imaging exercise instead.

VI Facilitating the process for our clients

> The big thing about this approach is how it allowed me to over-ride my "analytical and rational" left hemisphere and let my unconscious come up to the surface. There's no doubt that for me the image making was absolutely key to helping me override my thinking brain and access my more knowing self.
> Amelia, private client

When coaching with art, the following five stages form the basis of facilitating the process for our clients.

Stage 1. Imaging. Creating the space to allow images to present themselves to our client's inner eye. Allowing images to emerge without judgement or censorship (right hemisphere) rather than illustrations of thoughts (left hemisphere).

Stage 2. Creating. The client externalises their image and expresses themselves through making their art, trusting their intuition and instincts.

Stage 3. Connecting. Working alongside our client to facilitate their understanding and meaning of their image, connecting them to their art in a client-centred way.

Stage 4. Coaching. As the area of focus emerges and our client is clear about the area they want to work on, moving to coaching.

Stage 5. Continuing discoveries. From session to session and outside the sessions, noticing and making space for ongoing emerging themes, understanding and insights.

Stage 1. Imaging: allowing the image to emerge

The first step is imaging, a process that allows an image to emerge to our clients' inner eye, without censorship and judgement. It is about quieting the left hemisphere and allowing the right hemisphere to have a voice.

To start the process, we need to think about the space we are in. Ask yourself – will my client feel comfortable and safe working in this space? Will it be free of interruptions and private? Is it a space that will work for my client?

When the client is ready, we can introduce 'the mindfulness pause'. This creates a moment of calm, a meditative space that slows the pace down and brings the client to the present moment.

A mindfulness pause starts by asking the client to ensure they feel comfortable and supported in the chair they are sitting in, asking them to have both feet on the ground, with their hands relaxed in whatever way feels comfortable for them, then inviting them to soften their eyes or close them when they are ready. In my practice, I also shut my eyes as I take them through the mindfulness pause and the chosen exercise. It helps me to stay focused with them in the moment.

Once the client is comfortable, bring them to their breath by asking them to notice their natural pattern of breathing in and breathing out. Continue this for a few minutes. However, thoughts are never far away. Ask your client to notice theirs, to not get drawn into them, but rather just notice and come back to their breath. The mindfulness pause is about helping the client to become fully present and relaxed before introducing the imaging exercise. If you are not familiar with mindfulness, attending a mindfulness course will help to develop your skill and approach to creating and slowing down the pace for your clients. For more information, please see the References and Further Resources section at the end of the book.

Slowing the pace down helps the left hemisphere to relinquish the task, giving the right hemisphere the opportunity to take over.

When introducing and guiding someone through an exercise (see section IV), it is important to leave lots of pauses, giving space for images to emerge to our client's inner eye, in their own time. Remember, the left hemisphere dislikes things to be too slow and will try and come in quickly to get on with it. As the coach we may also feel uncomfortable with this slower pace – feeling we have got to get on with it too. Notice it and let it go. It will be your left hemisphere wanting to take over!

In this imaging space we want our clients to relinquish thinking, so it is important we banish the word when talking about the exercise, including the words 'think' and 'thought'. Thinking is a left-hemisphere activity, as we think in words. We want our clients to trust in whatever comes up and go with their intuition and instinct. For example, 'let an image come up' rather than 'what are you thinking about?'

It is important the image is uncensored, not judged or thought about. If an image is a thought image, it is just an illustration of a thought. If it is censored and judged, it is not going to be the issue.

When introducing the imaging we might use phrases such as:

'Without censoring, allow an image to float up of. . .' then pause for a few minutes to allow our client to do this.

'Trusting yourself, and without censoring, what image comes up for you when I say. . .' then pausing for a few minutes.

For a guided image, start to tell the story with enough pauses at each stage of the story so your client can image. See the example of going for an interview in Section v (see pages 72–78).

Once you have come to the end of the exercise and have given your client enough time to allow images to emerge for them, you could say: 'When you are ready, gently open your eyes and capture your image in whatever way you choose using the materials in the room [pause]'.

Sometimes the mindfulness pause doesn't work and it isn't always appropriate for the situation. It can take time for the mind to settle and the left hemisphere to relinquish control. In these circumstances, the 'just-draw-it!' exercise can be used. The spontaneity of it, the not thinking about it, seems to allow the right hemisphere to take over. The free exercise or play approach can work well too. The resulting images from these two approaches can be just as powerful.

Stage 2. Creating: externalising the image

I never knew what was going to emerge, although at times I was strangely conscious of very definite features or aspects that needed to feature in what I created.

Sam, director of a professional organisation

Once the client is ready to start externalising their image, in whatever way they choose, it is important we stand back and give them the space to do this. As the coach, our role is to observe and notice our client's image making process, whilst also being there for support if needed.

I usually stand or sit to one side, so I am not in the way, whilst still being able to see what they are doing. It is important we notice what materials they are using, how they make decisions, how they use the materials and how the image is created, noticing their process of art making for later exploration.

The support we offer should only be around the materials, answering any questions they may have. It is important we don't get things for our client as this would be our choice and not theirs. I remember in the early stages of working this way, handing a large piece of paper to a client, only to be met with confusion and them saying they would have chosen a smaller piece, but they would use it anyway. I had influenced their choice!

During the creating stage of the process your client may or may not talk. Some of my clients remain silent until they have finished, and others talk. This talk does not necessarily involve me and I only engage with them if invited to do so. Asking questions and talking during the externalising process can interfere with the emerging image and the right-hemisphere voice, reducing its potential. This is particularly so if working with groups. In this situation I always ask everyone, at the end of the imaging stage, to work in silence and I will actively quieten people who chatter.

Sometimes at the beginning of creating a client may say that an image hasn't come to mind. Here, ask if a colour or a shape has emerged, and if not, invite them to hold what they are feeling and to give themselves permission to allow their intuition to take over, creating whatever feels instinctively right. This often leads to powerful abstract images of self-expression. Many of the images shared in this book are abstract or partly abstract.

For example, when Sam had finished her imaging exercise that resulted in her breakthrough image of a curl (Colour Image 2, plate section), she didn't have an image, but rather a feeling of colours. 'I had absolutely no idea what was going to happen when I started painting, but I knew it began with orange. . . and then I added yellows and other orange tones, and yes, some pink.'

Clients need enough time to externalise their image. How long this takes will vary from image to image and usually takes no more than ten minutes. Your client will know when they are finished. However, even though they have finished, as you start to explore their image, you may find your client changes it, developing it as they go deeper into their inner world – the image continuing to emerge.

When James created his image in his second session, he took an A1 piece of paper and drew two lines that crossed – one from left to right and one from top to bottom, intersecting at the centre. When he had finished and was exploring his image, James then cut the image into four, creating a new image (Figures 7.2 and 7.3).

Figure 7.2 James' first image from his second coaching session

Figure 7.3 James' new image, created from cutting up and adding to his first image

Externalising from the client's perspective

James's reflections on his externalising of his images gives a wonderful insight into the image making process from the client's perspective:

> 'Anna asked me to draw the answer to the question: What does the need for discipline in writing feel like? What emerged was a strong black charcoal cross on a large piece of paper, and as I made it I felt the soft resistance of the charcoal and the grain of the paper transfer into my upper arm and noticed that the powdery residue at the edge of the lines was lovely – a byproduct which was more interesting than the object I had focused on creating. Then in another exercise I used two water-colours and noticed the watery fronds I had created as a byproduct as well. This led me to realise in a new way the importance of the activity rather than the looked-for meaning. The message seemed to be: Enjoy the process of writing and focus on that rather than the discipline.'

Stage 3. Connecting: discovering meaning

Once our client is ready to start exploring their image, we need to create, through curiosity, a space for our client to reflect, explore, interpret and come up with their own insights and stories around their imagery and the process they used to create it.

The client's image making process is as important as the image. The process is not only the choices made about what materials to use; it is also the physical process of creating and the order in which things happen. All of this is part of accessing what is really going on for someone. The physicality of the process links to the emotions involved, and the order of things can link to the relationships between things. When exploring the process, we are talking about the 'howness' of it: the energy of the marks, the feeling of it, the physical process. As James said when reflecting on his programme, 'Anna's observation on the way I was making marks, not just of the marks, parallels the process of much good coaching (not just "what did the client say?" but "how did she say it?").'

When connecting, the role of the coach is to notice without interpretation, facilitating the client's exploration. We are connecting the client to their image and giving them the space to allow their meanings and insights to emerge in their own time. The coach does not interpret the image or offer suggestions. As Amelia said about her sessions, 'I like the way Anna just observes and points things out that I have done – and the order I've done them in – rather than make assumptions about what might be going on.'

Through our facilitation, clients can deepen their awareness and understanding, unlock the hidden and shift their perceptions. This in turn leads to greater personal understanding, personal growth and ultimately change. As Jaye said, 'Anna was always on hand to help explore what to the untrained eye might look like to be a series of lines and squiggles but to me evolved into a definite plan of action.'

When exploring a clients' image, it is best to sit alongside them with their art in front of you both and take a person-centred approach, working with the belief that the person knows best, that the individual can reach their own potential when working in a climate of acceptance, congruence and empathy. This is at the heart of coaching and is one of the core principles for coaching with art, as explained in the previous chapter.

Through this approach we create a connection between the client and their image. We do this by holding up a mirror to our client through what we notice and observe about their image and their image making process. We do this whilst being mindful not to put our own reflections in that mirror, by not interpreting, problem solving or judging. If we do this, we reduce our client's ability to see the image for themselves.

It is important we ask our clients where they are in the image so the image is connected to them at a personal level. Clients can often start talking about their images in the third person, as though the image is completely detached from themselves.

For example, in Sam's first session, when she had completed her image I asked her where she was in the image. Sam realised she wasn't there, and she said that it 'prompted a mini-emotional reaction that I couldn't possibly have anticipated.'

After a while Sam knew exactly how to represent herself, adding and amending her image to capture it. It was connecting Sam to her image that led Sam to have early insights into her feelings about her role in the organisation and her feelings of 'otherness' – the core issue, as it turned out, for Sam.

When exploring the image together it is important you are creating the space for your client to reflect and talk. One of the most effective ways to do this is to ask as few (if any) questions as possible and just to offer observations and what you notice. Interestingly, questions are more left-hemisphere-orientated as they invite analysis, whereas just noticing and observing just holds the image, which is more aligned to right-hemisphere working.

For example, rather than ask 'I was wondering why you used yellow for the flowers', which is both a question and interpretive ('flowers'), you could say 'you used yellow here', indicating the area of the image where yellow has been used. This holds the space and is completely neutral.

You can also use your client's language. So, in the above example, if your client had described the image as a flower, then you could too. What's important is that you are not bringing in your own interpretation.

If your client asks a question of you, try not to be drawn in to answering; rather, hold the space and reflect back.

When exploring and making connections, we use the language of the art itself – the colours, marks made, relationship and size of images and objects, textures, the media used and so forth. This approach enables clients to get to a deeper level of awareness and meaning without having to analyse it. It allows the client to stay with the right-hemisphere way of being, allowing meaning to emerge without the need to label or explain it. As long as our client understands, we don't have to, and we don't need to have it explained to us. Meaning can be held in the language of art.

In an earlier example (Chapter 4, 'Coaching-with-art example: giving the silent right hemisphere a voice'), where a workshop participant, who was being coached, started to make marks using a blue colouring pencil, the coach did not ask 'what does the blue mean?' but rather just noticed the blue. By staying with the language of the image, meaning emerged for the client when it was ready. In this particular example, it represented values.

When talking about an image and the externalising process, we may find our client becoming less self-conscious, and the words they use becoming more spontaneous and uncensored. These can be words that your client needs to hear and could have significance to the area you are working on together.

Some examples of process 'questions'

Size/colour of paper, the materials used:

- you took a large white sheet
- you took a blue sheet
- you tore it in half

- this is the only part you did in red
- you have used a lot of green

Position and size:

- you put yourself on the edge of the page
- this shape is different to that shape
- this shape is small compared to the others
- these shapes overlap
- there is a lot of space between these shapes

The order of things:

- I noticed you made the yellow marks before you made the pink ones
- after you drew that shape, you added thicker lines around this other image
- you overlaid the red with purple
- you started in this corner, then moved to the other corner, before you put the green marks between them

Line making:

- this shape is coloured in
- this has a thicker line
- you use dots here
- this is very jagged

Noticing what is missing:

- in your house, I notice there are no windows [where the client has already identified the image as a house]
- you have left this part blank
- there is a gap in the middle
- I can't see a tail [where the client has identified the image as an animal or you had guided them to draw an animal]

Physicality:

- I noticed you put a lot of energy into those marks
- you made those marks quite tentatively
- you got hold of the clay and slammed it down
- you've done a lot of blending and softening
- you stood up

Wider reflections:

- you drew your colleague in red paint, yourself in grey chalk
- last time you used only green, this week there is no green

- you have used pastels each time you have drawn
- you use blue for work and yellow for home

Unlike words, which we can forget, the picture keeps. We can refer to it, know at once what it means and relate change to it. It is a safe, memorable and accurate way to share personal discoveries.

Stage 4. Coaching: working with the outcome

The outcome, issue or aha! moment can emerge quickly from an art-based exercise. Once it does, we move into coaching, just as we do with any other tool or technique we employ. The difference is that the image can remain central to the conversation and the language will include the language of art.

However, the image may also be put to one side and it may become more appropriate to bring in other coaching approaches. For example, when exploring Sam's 'otherness' we had conversations around Myers Briggs preferences and how to manage personal boundaries. With Jaye, I would often move to exploration of the issue through questioning, reflecting back and challenge.

Sometimes we don't need to do anything else as the art has done its work, and our client just knows. A transformational shift has happened.

As you coach, your client may want to add to or change their image in some way, or you can invite them to if they start to indicate that something needs amending or is not quite right now they have reflected on it.

In addition, as you coach your client might want to create another image or you may feel that another art-based exercise is appropriate, perhaps to explore new insights or new possibilities that have emerged. My clients can produce just one image in a session or many. There is no right or wrong, only what is right for the client and their session.

Stage 5. Continuing discoveries

One of the great things about working with art is that the images clients create keep on giving and there is ongoing and continuing discovery.

One of the most valuable ways in which images keep on giving is through emerging themes and patterns.

As you work with your client, they will produce a number of images. As they do you may start to notice patterns and themes. These may be invaluable observations to bring to the client as they may raise something new, reinforce the importance of something, unlock something or bring a shift. Themes and patterns could be specific recurring images; they could be colours, a particular type of mark or the materials used. They may include the way a client depicts themselves or someone else, or the relationships between things.

It is also important for your client to have the opportunity to notice themes and patterns for themselves. Having previous images available, laying them out so your client can look at them side by side, will open up possibilities for new connections.

For example, when Sam looked back at her coaching programme, she reflected on her theme of circles: 'I have often wondered about all of the circles. It became clear in the final session. Armadillo-like, the circles are curled up balls of protection. A very closed world in #1, with my own little protective circle struggling to break into the organisational closed circle. My curl in #2 retains its curves, but is less tightly balled – starting to unfurl, if you like – but I am surrounded by tightly curled balls. . .'

Having images available from previous sessions also gives clients the opportunity to develop their images or change them if they want to.

For example, when Amelia was reviewing her images as part of her final session, she was strongly drawn to an image she wanted to change. 'Of all the images I had done there was one that I was particularly drawn to and I wanted to make some changes to it. . . There were a few things that I really did want to change. Most strong was wanting to make the tree feel more rooted, and to have leaves and colour in it. Now I think it is a beautiful image. . .'

There may also be times when a client does not know why they have included a colour, a mark or a form and they don't know what it means. This is okay, as meaning may emerge later, when it is ready to be known.

For example, in Sam's final image she had included some flowers, and in the session Sam did not know why. Later, when looking back at the image and reflecting on the session, Sam said: 'It has taken me until this moment of writing to realise that the flowers represent growth.'

Images keep on giving. There is an ongoing and continual discovery!

VII Managing ourselves in this process

The role of the coach in coaching with art is to create a safe, confidential and supportive space for our clients so they can image, create and connect to their art. Through their externalised visual images, we facilitate their exploration of their externalised image so they can access the hidden and deepen their awareness and understanding in a way that can lead to greater insights and understanding. We need to manage this space and we need to manage ourselves in the process.

One of the core principles of coaching with art is being person-centred. As explained in chapter 6, this is because when we are working in a person-centred way we are putting our clients first, with the belief that the person knows best, that the individual can reach their own potential when working in a climate of acceptance, congruence and empathy. If we are not working in this way, our own agenda may be influencing our client's experience. As a result, we need to be aware of our own patterns that may be affecting our ability to be person-centred, and how they may be affecting our coaching practice.

When working in a person-centred way we are in effect holding up the mirror to our client without putting our own reflection in it. However, it can be very easy

88 Coaching with art in practice

```
         Persecutor                    Rescuer
                  \                   /
                   \                 /
                    \               /
                     \             /
                      \           /
                       \         /
                        \       /
                         \     /
                          \   /
                           \ /
                          Victim
```

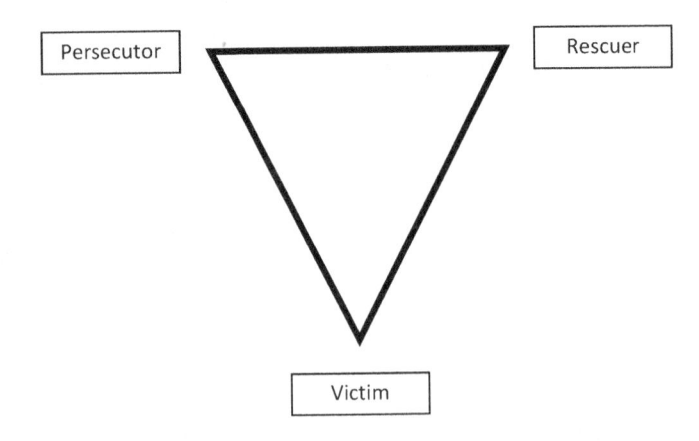

Figure 7.4 The Karpman Drama Triangle

and tempting when coaching with art to interpret and offer judgements on what you see in front of you. I always think it is far more tempting to do this with visual language than it is for verbal.

If we do, why are we? What role are we actually playing? And is it helping our client? We need to be alert to our own patterns and behaviours.

Karpman's Drama Triangle is a good basis on which to reflect on our patterns and whether we are being person-centred. None of the roles in the Karpman Drama Triangle (Figure 7.4) are person-centred. The persecutor judges, the rescuer solves the problem, the victim gives up her power to someone else. If, as coaches, we are in the triangle, we know we are not being person-centred.

For example, with the person-centred approach a coach does not, in the main, answer questions. Instead, they reflect them back so the client can discover for themselves that they know the answer. By doing this the coach does not keep the client in victim-mode (by answering their question) but enables them to become empowered. This is mirrored by the noticing and observing that the coach does when facilitating their client's exploration of their image. Only the client knows what the image means to them. It is the coach's role to help them discover it.

Take a moment to reflect on your own practice. What patterns might you have or what roles might you be playing that may be putting you – and, by default, your client – in the Drama Triangle?

For example, are you the victim?

- Are you worrying whether your client thinks you are professional or not if you use this approach?
- Do you need your client to like you and think you are a good coach?

- Are you worrying about the materials or the process and looking to your client to reassure you?
- Are you seeking approval from your client about the space or whether you are doing a good job?

Are you rescuing your client?

- Are you reassuring your client that their image is okay?
- Do you get things for your client, meaning to be helpful?
- Do you placate them by saying everyone feels as they do?
- Do you reassure them by saying that you feel the same?
- Do you feel the need to solve your client's problems?

Are you persecuting your client? (Albeit unintentionally.)

- Perhaps you are inadvertently telling them what to do. ('Why don't you use. . .')
- Is your client asking you to make judgments and you inadvertently are? ('Your image is okay. . .')
- Is the client putting you in the persecutor role with comments like 'it's okay for you' and you reinforce this by how you respond?
- Perhaps you are telling them that it is easy to do ('everyone can do it'), making them feel like a victim?

If you are starting to recognise some of your own patterns, what would you like to do to explore and work on them?

VIII Boundaries and ethics

As coaches we know that we coach within our boundaries, and issues may come up that fall outside of them, issues that may need to be referred to another professional, such as a counsellor, therapist or general practitioner.

We may also find things arise that fall outside of the contracted-for programme. We need to be aware when this happens so we can either bring a session back to the coaching purpose or discuss changes and re-contract.

As we have seen, coaching with art can work at a deep level, tapping into the unconscious. As a result, we may find our clients starting to make visible experiences and memories that have stayed hidden for a long time. These may be areas that a client does not want to go to, is not ready for and may be outside of the coaching boundary. We need to be alert to this. We can do this through our own reflective practice and by talking our work through with our supervisors. We must always ensure we work within our capabilities, do our best for our clients and refer where appropriate. If you are ever in doubt, check in with your supervisor.

It is important that we have real and clear intent behind the work we do, contract fully and are alert to straying into therapeutic spaces.

IX The final session and closing out

As with the first session, the final session and closing out of an art-based coaching programme needs to be considered.

With all coaching we should close out well, leaving our clients in a place of confidence and empowerment to continue and grow. It is also a time for reflection and evaluation, not only on the success of the programme, but also for our clients, for them to take stock and recognise how far they may have come.

The final session in a coaching-with-art programme provides a rich space for both the client's reflections as well as the review of the programme. First, in the final session we are able to bring together all the images our client has created, giving them the opportunity to consolidate their coaching experience. The final session:

- gives the client a final opportunity to look at any emerging themes and patterns together with the coach
- gives the client a visual record of progress made, including new insights, aha! moments and significant changes; they can easily go back to how it felt at the beginning and articulate their progress through the language of their images; this can reinforce their confidence and be very empowering
- allows for the success of the programme to be discussed with the coach and can provide some very tangible measures

Second, the final session provides the opportunity for our clients to do a closing imaging exercise. This image could be focused on 'what next', or the future, as well as how it feels right now. Again, the exercise will depend on what feels right in the final session with your client. These final images can be very empowering, leaving them with a real sense of 'what next'.

All the case study clients in this book who have had coaching programmes did final images.

Final images from the case studies

Jaye's final image

For Jaye, her final image brought together all the different materials she used across all of her images. This image (Colour Image 9, plate section) represents her energy, ideas and possibilities from her research, together with the many different ways that Jaye is writing about and communicating her research.

James' final image

James created three images, all related to his coaching programme (shown together in Colour Image 7, plate section). The final of these

(continued)

(continued)

three (shown separately in Colour Image 13, plate section) looks to James' future. James said that 'the creation of the final simple image to accompany me on the next stage of my journey was a huge benefit.'

Sam's final image

Sam's final image focused on her future (Colour Image 14, plate section); 'This was the image I drew of my future. It is unclear exactly what the future might look like, but hopefully it will provide me with a sense of completeness and fulfilment.'

Amelia's final image

Amelia took a previous image and amended it as her final image (Colour Image 4, plate section). Amelia summed up her final image: 'I felt it summed up what my life was becoming and how I wanted my life to be. . . Random – no straight lines – go with the flow – no borders – off the page – full of colour, love and music. What a wonderful thing to aspire to. It feels really exciting and beautiful.'

****

A final thought before closing the chapter about taking coaching with art further: once you feel confident with coaching with art, why not start to use it as a space where your clients can experiment?

Experiments are used to raise awareness, gain insight and try new ways of being, taking risks in a safe place. You could use the five steps for coaching with art to explore art-based exercises around 'what-if' or 'how-would-it' scenarios.

The possibilities are exciting, and I am always learning!

Chapter 8

Materials

'I actually loved the process and experience of using the materials, especially the big chunky sticks and flicking the watercolour paint . . . I noticed an almost childlike enjoyment of playing with the various materials and colours.'
Amelia, private client

The one area I haven't yet spoken about in any detail is the materials we bring into an art-based coaching session. As you will have seen from the case studies, I offer a variety of materials as this is an important part of my clients' self-expression. Self-expression, and therefore insight, comes not just through the image but also through the different colours used, the use of one type of material against another, different textures, different sizes of paper, the mix of collage and paint and so forth. In the words of one client, 'I found . . . having access to all manner of materials liberating, calming and energising' (Jaye, consultant).

In this chapter, I look at the different mediums and supports you can use to create visual imagery, explaining them and their suitability and where to buy them. New materials are coming onto the market all the time, so I have focused on the most well-known and easily available.

A medium is anything that is used to create marks and imagery such as pens, pencils, paints or clay, and supports are anything on which we create those images, such as paper, card and canvas. There are many different types of mediums and supports and if you are new to using art and creative materials it can be a little overwhelming. To help you make your choices of what to offer I look at:

- supports
- drawing mediums
- painting and water-based mediums
- other mediums, including clay and collage
- accessories
- storing your materials
- where to buy

In Chapter 9, where I talk about getting started, I provide guidance on putting a starter pack together as well as making a portable pack.

Supports

Cartridge paper

This paper is used for drawing with graphite pencils, graphite sticks, charcoal and coloured pencils. It can also be used for pastels and collage work. Cartridge paper comes in weights such as 120 or 150 gsm. The heavier it is, the thicker it is, meaning it can take more punishment! Cartridge paper can be bought in pads of A5, A4, A3 and A2 size, as well as in sheets up to A1, the largest size. Cartridge paper is usually in white or cream, but can be found in other colours, particularly at lighter weights.

Card

Card is available in all sorts of colours and all sorts of sizes, from A5 to A1 (smallest to biggest) and in a variety of thicknesses. Card can be used as a support on which to create images, and it can also be cut up and folded to collage or create 3D images.

Watercolour paper

As the name suggests, this paper is used for painting in watercolour, and can also be used for acrylic paint, poster paint, inks and water-based drawing mediums such as water-soluble coloured pencils, Inktense sticks and watercolour sticks. This paper comes in three surfaces: 'hot-pressed', which is very smooth, 'not', which has a slight texture to it, and 'rough', which is highly textured. This paper is also sold in different gsm weights, colours and sizes. It is available in different-sized pads as well as sheets which can be cut to size.

Pastel paper

This is a specially textured paper, often in a myriad of colours, which is used for soft and hard pastels. It has a fine surface a bit like sandpaper to hold the layers of pigment on the surface.

Canvas

This is a material-based support that can come in ready-stretched sizes and different shapes. Here, the canvas is stretched over wooden frames and stapled into place. It is also primed with a coat of white base so that it is ready for use. This is the most straightforward way of buying canvases if you decide you want to offer these to your client. Canvases are used with oil, acrylics and water-based oil paints. You can also buy canvas on a roll and cut it and stretch it yourself, but this gets fiddly and I would recommend using the readymade ones for art-based sessions. By their nature, the larger sizes are not that portable.

Acrylic and oil paper

As an alternative to canvases, there are papers available specifically for acrylic and oil paints. They come in pads from A5 to A2 and have a specially prepared surface to enable them to take these paints.

Drawing mediums

Graphite pencils and sticks

These are your classic drawing tools that are essentially graphite grey. They range from very hard (H9) to very soft (B9). The softer the pencil, the broader and darker the marks you make; the harder the pencil, the finer and lighter the marks. The standard pencil we use is HB. Pencils and graphite sticks can be bought singly or in a tin with a range of hard to soft. These drawing pencils can create a myriad of marks and can be blended using purpose blenders, a piece of tissue or your finger. They can also be erased and smudged using hard or soft erasers.

Colouring pencils

These are standard pencils with a range of colours in a pack and which we all probably used as children when drawing at school and at home. They make quite fine detailed lines, can be used for shading and can be blended in the same way as graphite pencils, above. By layering the colours, you can create other colours and effects. They are hard to erase.

Felt-tip pens

Again, we will be familiar with these as a standard art tool for children and adults alike! These come in a range of colours, which when used are quite intense. There is also a range of nib thicknesses, from very fine to very fat. They cannot be blended or erased but can colour in big areas if you use the larger ones, and colours can be overlaid to create new colours.

Wax crayons

These are waxy crayons, as the name suggests, and again we will have used these as children. They come in multicolour packs of varying numbers and sizes and create less-detailed pieces of work. They create waxy thick marks and can be layered to create different colours and effects.

Pastels

These are a chalky drawing medium that come in square and round sticks. They can be hard or soft and have a myriad of available colours. Pastels can be layered over each other, blended as a single colour and used for linear chalky, textured marks. They come in a variety of pack sizes, as well as singly. When used, the images are easy to smudge, so, when finished, the image should be fixed using a pastel and charcoal fixative spray. You can also use hairspray.

Oil pastels

These are sticks of waxy pigment that create thick, buttery colours. They come in many colours and can be bought in a variety of pack sizes as well as singly. They can be layered to create effects and colours and will need a special blending medium applied with a cloth to create softer marks.

Charcoal

Charcoal is charred black wood and is available in sticks of different thicknesses and hardness. The mark making is broad and soft and lends itself to larger work. It is difficult to work in detail with this medium. To remove charcoal, you need to use an eraser – a putty rubber is best. As with pastels, charcoal work needs to be fixed with a pastel and charcoal fixative otherwise the image smudges and can disappear. You can also buy charcoal pencils, coloured charcoals and large coloured charcoal blocks. These colours are muted and limited in range.

Painting and water-based mediums

To work with paints and water-based mediums you will need to have brushes available of varying sizes and water, as well as a good weight of paper to take the paint. The brush should be appropriate for the medium and you can buy watercolour, acrylic and oil paint brushes. If you are using traditional oil paints, you will also need the right cleaner for them as they are not water-soluble.

Watercolour

This is the classic water-based paint and comes in tubes and pans. Pans are the hard square paints that you find in watercolour paint tins. There are many makes and colours and starter paint tins with a selection of standard colours are available from art shops. This is an expressive medium that is quite hard to control, but very portable. My clients get drawn to these paints and enjoy the freedom of expression they create.

Acrylic

This is a fast-drying water-based paint that comes in tubes and pots. It can be very colourful as well as very subtle and, once dry, can be painted over, unlike watercolours. This is a very popular paint to work with as it is very forgiving and dries quickly. However, it isn't very portable.

Oil paints

There are two types of oil paints: traditional and water-based. These paints take a long time to dry and I wouldn't necessarily recommend them for art in coaching.

Water-soluble pencils and colour sticks

There are now a whole host of solid water-based pencils, pens and sticks that when water is added create lovely painterly marks. These are very portable and could be a good alternative to offering paint. These mediums include: watercolour pencils and sticks, Inktense pencils and sticks and water-soluble fibre pens. They all come in a large range of colours and can be bought individually as well as in packs and tins of different quantities. The range of water-soluble sticks and pens is evolving all the time and well worth keeping an eye on.

Other mediums

Clay

This is a lovely tactile medium for creating 3D images. It is worth exploring craft shops for a non-wet clay which can come in other colours and can be air dried. You could also use children's modelling clay. You need to consider the time clay or similar materials take to dry and where your clients' creations can be safely left to harden.

Play dough

This is a children's 'clay' (Play-Doh) that comes in different colours and is designed to be reused rather than hardened to make permanent sculptures or models. It is composed of flour, water, salt, boric acid and mineral oil. You can also make your own, which can be baked and hardened. This is usually referred to as 'play dough'.

Collage

Collage can be made up of all sorts of materials, not just sticking pictures torn out of magazines onto card. A range of papers, fabrics, shapes etc. can be built up through collecting found objects around your home, from packaging and from friends. You can also buy lots of collage material from craft shops. The choice is endless. To do collage you also need to ensure you have the correct size of card, glue, scissors and other accessories that will work with the materials you are offering.

Accessories

In this category, I include all those things that you may need to help with the image making exercise. This may include:

- pencil sharpeners
- scissors
- glue
- kitchen paper towels and wet wipes for cleaning hands and tidying up
- brushes
- water pots – you can get collapsible versions of these that make them portable
- mixing palette for paints
- paperclips
- sticky tape
- elastic bands to roll up images and make them easy for you or your client to carry
- fixative for pastel and charcoal work or hairspray
- erasers

This is not an exhaustive list and your accessories will need to match the materials you choose to offer. If you forget something, don't worry, as sometimes improvisation can lead to unexpected conversations and insights!

Storing your materials

As well as having materials on offer, you also need to think about where you will store them. I have a dedicated large box for materials that sits underneath the table. I also have a couple of large portfolio cases for storing papers. Portfolios can be cheap and come in A4 to A1 sizes. They have handles for carrying and a strap for putting over your shoulder. I also have a trolley when transporting materials to my workshops.

Where to buy

Art materials can be bought almost anywhere these days. There are art and craft shops, both on the high street and online. If you are uncomfortable going into an art shop, shops such as WHSmith, Paperchase and Hobbycraft have a good selection of the basics. Most good stationers will have basic accessories and materials too. Toy shops are also a good place to explore.

At the back of the book, I have listed some links to online art shops where you can explore what's on offer and request catalogues that you can browse at your leisure.

If you are unsure of what to offer, I would suggest buying one or two of something. Good art shops and online shops enable you to buy just one of a material, such as a pastel stick or tube of watercolour paint. You can then try them out before investing in a pack of 24. Art shops will also have trial packs of papers available to buy that include different colours, weights and textures.

****

The best way to work out what mediums and supports you want to use in your practice is to experiment and find out about them for yourself. I would encourage you to just play and make marks, testing out what you can do with them and their limits, how you can mix them up and those that work well together and those that don't. In the next chapter, I have suggested some exercises to help you do this.

Chapter 9

Getting started

> *'I underestimated the personal value/benefit I would get from [coaching with art]... the power of it has stayed with me and the curiosity of how it works.'*
> Cathy, coach and workshop participant

In this chapter, I share with you the things I have learnt along the way that may help you to get started with coaching with art. In Chapter 5, I explored some of the biggest barriers coaches can put up to coaching this way. If you are experiencing some of these and want to get over them, I have included some suggestions for helping you build confidence in your own creativity as well as some hints and tips around building confidence in your practice.

Other suggestions for getting started have come from the questions I get asked by coaches who want to coach with art, and the challenges those who have been on my workshops share with me when trying to get started.

In this chapter, I cover:

- building confidence in your own creativity
- developing your confidence in coaching with art
- being prepared
- materials
    - putting a starter pack together
    - making a portable pack

Building confidence in your own creativity

One of the biggest barriers for coaches who want to work in this way is their own confidence in being a creative person. In Chapter 5, I invited you to explore your own art story and encouraged you to hold your insights with curiosity and without judgement. If, when you did this exercise, you had some strong negative perceptions about yourself as a creative person, it is important for you to work on this. How can we ask our clients to work in this way, if we do not feel confident ourselves?

If this is an area you want to develop, the following suggestions will start to help you to explore and build confidence in and value your own creativity.

Playing!

The first thing to do is to give yourself permission to play and be curious. Whatever you do in the following exercises doesn't have to be shared with anyone and it is not there to be judged. The only person who would do that is you. If you find your inner judgement creeping in, notice it and let it go.

First, get lots of paper. This can be printer or photocopy paper. The cheaper it is, the better, as it won't feel daunting to use it.

Next, get colouring pens and pencils, crayons – anything you have to hand in the house. But not flipchart markers or whiteboard pens. If you want to try something new or don't have much in the house, buy what you are instinctively drawn towards. Don't censor your choices. Then, when you are ready, and are in a space where you aren't going to be interrupted and have the time to relax and just be:

- fill one piece of paper with the colour you are most drawn to
- fill another piece of paper with the colour you least like
- taking each different medium you have (crayons, pencils, paints etc.), fill a piece of paper with each one, any way you want to
- on another piece of paper, see how many different sorts of marks you can make – lines, dots, squiggles, shading, thick marks, thin marks. . .
- on some other pieces of paper, mix up the different mediums you have. For example, what happens if you put colouring pencil down first and then put wax crayons on the top? Just keep on experimenting. . . have fun!
- how about trying a bigger or smaller piece of paper? If you are using A4, you can stick sheets together to create bigger sheets or you can tear one in half to create an A5 sheet. How did it feel to work bigger or smaller?
- try making marks with your eyes closed
- make fast marks, make slow marks
- stand up, sit down, work on the floor. . . whatever feels right for you

When you have finished, take a moment to reflect on how you feel. Often, we have a childlike joy in working this way. What did you particularly enjoy doing?

If, whilst playing, you couldn't quieten your judgements of what you were doing, what do you want to do to help you let them go?

Looking at all the pieces of paper in front of you, is there one (or more) that you are particularly drawn to? What is it about that piece that attracts you?

What do you want to do with all your creativity?

This play exercise is a creative way of having some fun, loosening up and relieving tensions. It is also a great way to familiarise yourself with the materials you want to offer to your clients.

Keeping a visual journal

Another way of introducing creativity into your day is to keep a visual diary. This is a notebook in which you record your day visually. You could draw something, paint something, stick something in and elaborate on it. . . whatever you want that captures your day. It could be an event in that day or something that sums up how you feel about that day. It doesn't have to be something real either. You may be having a blue day or a yellow day and decide to fill a page with blue or yellow. It could be something abstract, a shape, a swirl and kaleidoscope of marks, a mix of collage. Just let your intuition and imagination loose.

When you've finished your image, pause for a moment and make a note next to it of what the image conjures up for you.

Remember: this journal is yours. It does not have to be shared with anyone unless you choose to do so.

Trying something new

Developing our creativity comes with trying things out. Is there something that you have always wanted to do? Is there something that you find yourself drawn to? Have you been addicted to the television programmes about baking, sewing or pottery? This is your inner creative voice nudging you to give it a go.

Take the plunge, book that course and have a go at something new. Most of the other participants will be new to it too.

Some ideas:

- making books
- gardening
- baking
- sugar work
- sculpture
- stone masonry
- print making
- rug making
- metal work and blacksmithing
- pottery
- knitting
- sewing
- paper cutting
- origami

As coaches, one of our roles is to provide stretch for our clients. It is our role to offer challenge and to take them a little (and sometimes a lot) out of their comfort zones. This is where growth and confidence lies. If we don't do this for ourselves from time to time, what role model are we setting for our clients?

Reading a book or two

There are two books I highly recommend in helping to find your creativity. The first is Julia Cameron's *The Artist's Way* (1995). It is aimed at anyone who wants to discover and recover their creative self. It is a programme of activities over 12 weeks that helps you find your own path to creativity. It isn't just for artists.

The other book is Betty Edwards' *The New Drawing on the Right Side of the Brain* (2001). This book helps anyone who wants to draw – even those who think they can't! There is a wonderful exercise in the book where the author shares an image and asks you to draw it and then to draw it upside-down. The difference is remarkable. I have done this exercise and it proved to me how the brain can really interfere with drawing and being able to capture what we are really seeing. If you have always wanted to draw, then this book is a great starting place to build your confidence in your ability.

Developing your confidence in coaching with art

As with all coaching, the way to develop your confidence in coaching with art is practice. This is crucial for deepening your understanding of this approach and to develop your way of working with art.

This can come in many forms, including:

- being coached
- just practising – practise, practise, practise!
- supervision
- courses and development
- building a network of support

Being coached

When training as a coach and learning new approaches, it is often the experience of being the client that really helps to embed the learning. There is nothing like doing it yourself to build confidence when working with others. The same is for coaching with art. Through being coached, you will experience what it feels like to do an imaging process, then to externalise your image visually and talk about your image. Being coached opens up how deep the experience is for the client, what barriers may come up and what the whole experience feels like. It is only by being coached that we can then put ourselves into the shoes of our client.

Experiencing coaching with art as a client is one of the best ways of deepening your understanding of this approach and building your confidence in using it.

You could also consider setting up some peer co-coaching with someone who is also wanting to develop art as part of their practice.

Practise, practise, practise

It goes without saying that the more you practise, the greater your confidence will be. Through practice you will be able to develop your own style to coaching with art, build your own repertoire of exercises and notice your own patterns that may need managing.

How about:

- trying out coaching with art on some coaching colleagues who can offer you good constructive feedback (positive and developmental)?
- starting to introduce coaching with art in safer spaces, where you already have good rapport and trust with your clients?
- offering some trial sessions at a reduced cost, explaining you are learning and looking for feedback?
- introducing coaching with art in different scenarios so you can experience the many different coaching scenarios this approach can be used for? (It is often only our perceptions and fears that limit the possibilities of coaching with art.)

Whilst you are coaching, keep a reflective journal where you can record your approaches, what you tried, what worked well, what concerns you. Looking through will give you a wealth of information to help you shape your practice and be alert to potential development areas.

Supervision

Coaching with art works deeply and we may stray into areas outside of coaching, potentially putting our client into an unexpected situation. It is therefore important we have a safe, confidential space within which we can explore coaching in this way.

Supervision is an important part of our practice, keeping us alert to our developmental needs, the quality of our practice and boundary management. It helps to build and maintain our confidence in our practice as well as provide confidence to those who engage us.

Keeping a reflective journal will help you to develop your own internal supervisor, but it is also important to engage a supervisor to talk through your practice. It not only helps to build your confidence but also helps you to be alert to boundary and ethical issues that may come up when working so deeply.

Courses and development

There is nothing like being part of a workshop or group who are learning and developing this skill together to build confidence in your practice. These courses don't just have to be coaching-based; they could also be around art therapy, art in education and the community, as well as creative courses.

The most important thing is for the workshop or course to meet your needs and what you want to learn and experience for your personal and professional development.

Building a network of support

Coaching with art isn't that visible and you may feel unsupported in trying this approach out. To help build your confidence as well as your own development in this area, why not find other coaches in your area who are doing something similar and create a network of support for art-based coaching?

Being prepared

Being prepared in anything gives us confidence in what we do. In Chapter 7, I talked in detail about preparing for a coaching-with-art programme and individual sessions. Preparation is also important for giving confidence to our private and organisational clients.

Being prepared means:

- good and comprehensive contracting so you can manage expectations, ensure your client understands how the approach works and what happens in a session
- being really clear about the boundaries within which you use this approach and ensuring your client is aware of these through your contracting
- making sure the space you coach in is right for coaching with art
- you have a good selection of materials for your client to work with and you have checked them to ensure you have enough of everything and nothing needs refilling
- having an idea of the sorts of exercises you could use and how you would introduce them
- knowing you have enough time in the session to facilitate the creative process from imaging through to coaching
- knowing what you would do if your client decided they didn't want to work this way
- thinking through how you would manage a situation that was outside your boundaries or created an ethical dilemma for you
- giving yourself some reflective time to prepare yourself for the session, so you can be fully present and person-centred for your client

Having the above practicalities in hand and questions answered in your mind will help you increase your confidence in running a coaching-with-art session.

Getting started with materials

I am often asked what materials should be included in a pack for a coaching-with-art session. It can be easy to spend a lot of money on materials, so it is best to start with a good basic selection, adding to it as your practice builds. This section looks at putting a starter pack together, as well as making a portable one.

When putting together your materials you also need to consider if you are working in a dedicated space, where you can offer a wider choice, or whether you need to have a portable pack. If you are working in different locations, you will also need to consider what materials are suitable for that space. For example, some spaces may not welcome clients making a mess with paints.

Putting together a starter pack

When putting a pack together, think about the choice that is available to your client in terms of different colours, different textures, mark making and how big or small they can work. Is there enough choice for self-expression? Is there an alternative choice for easing them into working with art if they have reservations about creating an image?

The following list of materials is a starter-for-ten and is great if you are working from a dedicated space. However, you can start even smaller, with just some wax crayons, colouring pencils and chunky felt-tip pens. Add to this some different sizes of paper and a magazine, and you are away.

Starting a pack

- wax crayons
- colouring pencils and felt-tip pens
- a selection of pastels (sometimes called chalks) – include black and white
- chunky sticks of colour – large crayons, oil pastels or large chalks that make larger-than-life marks!
- paint box, such as a watercolour box
- play dough, modelling clay or something similar (not essential but great to offer sculpture if you can)
- coloured papers and/or card for cutting up
- old magazines for sourcing images for collage
- a selection of found materials, such as ribbons, tin foil, tissue paper and scraps of material and wrapping paper; you can build this over time, adding to it as and when you find something
- cartridge paper – buy an A2-sized pad as A2 sheets can be cut into A3 sheets (cutting in half), A4 sheets (cutting into quarters) and A5 sheets (by cutting the A4 sheets in half again). This means you only have to buy one pad and not several. 120gsm-weight is ideal as it is heavy enough for water-based materials such as watercolour paint
- glue and sticky tape
- scissors
- pencil sharpener and eraser
- fixative for the pastels – hairspray works well and is much cheaper!

- water pots for the water-based materials – I have jam jars and plastic soup containers, plus a collapsible pot for travelling
- brushes of different sizes for the paints
- kitchen roll and hand wipes
- something to store them all in
- an apron, just in case someone wants to start flicking paint around!

You also need to think about how your client is going to carry their art if they want to take it away with them. If they do take their art away, you will need, with permission, to be able to take a photo of it so you have it available at the next session if your client forgets to bring it along. Most of the time, I use my tablet or phone.

Making a portable pack

When putting a portable pack together, think about how you are travelling, what you are able to carry, what space is available to work in and any restrictions that may apply. Your pack may vary depending on the situation.

As a guide, I carry the following. First, my briefcase always contains:

- children's wax crayons – a pack of 24 so there are lots of colours to choose from
- felt-tip pens – a pack of 24 with lots of colours
- colouring pencils – a pack of 24
- sticky tape
- glue stick
- A4 paper
- pencil sharpener

This means that even if I wasn't planning on using an artbased approach, if it feels right and my client is open to it, I can run one.

Again, I also always have some means of taking a photo just in case my client makes art and wants to take it away with them. This is usually my phone or tablet. Don't forget to ask permission before taking photos of your clients' work.

If I am planning for coaching with art, I take with me an A2 portfolio case and a bag or brief case containing all the above, plus:

- a couple of magazines
- A3 and A2 paper
- coloured A4 paper – a few sheets
- Inktense sticks, which are water-soluble and can be used like a watercolour box – box of 24 colours
- a couple of sticks of charcoal for expressive, big mark making – people seem to love these
- pastels – a box of 12
- collapsible water pot

- watercolour brushes in a couple of different sizes
- kitchen roll and hand wipes
- some collage materials
- fixative
- a few elastic bands to roll up the images for my client to take away. If I take them away, I put them flat in my portfolio case

I don't take anything with me that will take time to dry, or lead to a creation that could be damaged in transit.

All the materials I use come in either flat tins or small boxes, which make them very easy to put into a bag, briefcase or alongside the paper in the portfolio bag. The accessories are kept in a pencil case. With the kitchen roll, I tear sheets off and fold them up so I don't need to take the cumbersome roll with me. Everything is neatly stored and I don't feel like a packhorse.

****

I hope this chapter has helped you to think about what you need to get started.

If you want to explore further, there are some useful websites and books to support the development of your own practice of coaching with art, some of which I have included in the References and Further Resources section at the back of the book.

I hope you find coaching with art as remarkable and rewarding as I do, and I would like to leave the final words of the book to one of my clients.

> I have been struck by the progress achieved through the medium of art. I'm sure I have unravelled things much more quickly than might otherwise have been the case. I have had coaching with Anna before . . . but bringing art into the equation seems to amplify her impact still further. I've found it incredibly powerful. I never cease to be amazed at what emerges apparently from nowhere. Clearly, art as a medium possesses a key to the unconscious that is definitely worth exploiting.
>
> Sam, director of a professional organisation

References

Edwards, Betty (2001). *The New Drawing on the Right Side of the Brain*. London: HarperCollins.

Cameron, Julia (1995). *The Artist's Way*. Basingstoke and Oxford: Pan Books.

References and further resources

Books, articles and online posts used as source materials in the book

Bush, Morgan (2013). 'Adrian Hill, UK Founder of Art Therapy'. London Art Therapy Centre. Retrieved from https://arttherapycentre.com/blog/adrian-hill-uk-founder-art-therapy-morgan-bush-intern/.

Cook, Jill (2013). *Ice-age Art: The Arrival of the Modern Mind*. London: The British Museum Press.

Edwards, Betty (2001). *The New Drawing on the Right Side of the Brain*. London: HarperCollins.

Gazzaniga, Michael S. (1998). 'The Split Brain Revisited'. *Scientific American*, July, pp. 51–55.

Gazzaniga, Michael S. and LeDoux, Joseph E. (1978). *The Integrated Mind*. New York: Plenum Press, pp. 148–149.

Gots, Jason (2012). 'Your Story Telling Brain'. *Bigthink*, 23 January. Retrieved from https://bigthink.com/overthinking-everything-with-jason-gots/your-storytelling-brain.

Haeyen, Suzanne, van Hooren, Susan and Hutschemaekers, Giel (2015). 'Perceived Effects of Art Therapy in the Treatment of Personality Disorders, Cluster B/C: A Qualitative Study'. *The Arts in Psychotherapy*, vol. 45 (September): pp. 1–10.

Jung, Carl (2009). *The Red Book: Liber Novus*. Edited by Sonu Shamdasani. New York: Philemon Foundation and W.W. Norton & Co.

Malchiodi, Cathy A. (2007). *The Art Therapy Sourcebook*. New York: McGraw-Hill.

Malchiodi, Cathy A. (2016). 'Why Art Therapy Works'. *Psychology Today*, 30 August. Retrieved from www.psychologytoday.com/gb/blog/arts-and-health/201608/why-art-therapy-works.

Malik, Kenan (2013). 'Divided Brain, Divided World?' *Pandaemonium* blog, 21 February. Retrieved from https://kenanmalik.wordpress.com/2013/02/21/divided-brain-divided-world/.

McGilchrist, Iain (2012). *The Master and His Emissary: The Divided Brain and the Making of the Western World*. Princeton, NJ: Yale University Press.

McLeod, Saul (2007). 'Carl Rogers'. *Simply Psychology*. Retrieved from www.simplypsychology.org/carl-rogers.html.

Psychology Today (2016). 'Review of *Finding Flow* by Mihaly Csiakszentmihalyi', 9 June. Retrieved from www.psychologytoday.com/gb/articles/199707/finding-flow.

Schacter, Daniel L. (2002). *The Seven Sins of Memory: How the Mind Forgets and Remembers*. Boston, MA: Houghton and Mifflin.

Silverstone, Liesl (1997). *Art Therapy the Person-Centred Way – Art and Development of the Person (2nd Edition)*. London: Jessica Kingsley.

Wikipedia (2016). Entry for 'Left-Brain Interpreter'. Retrieved from https://ipfs.io/ipfs/ QmXoypizjW3WknFiJnKLwHCnL72vedxjQkDDP1mXWo6uco/wiki/Left_brain_ interpreter.html.
Wikipedia (2017). Entry for 'Margaret Naumberg'. Retrieved from https://en.wikipedia. org/wiki/Margaret_Naumburg.

Further resources

The following books and links are for anyone who is looking for more information or wishes to buy materials online.

Websites

www.artincoaching.co.uk – The author's website and blog, with details of the workshops the author runs on coaching with art.
www.baat.org.uk – The British Association of Art Therapists website, with information and resources for anyone interested in or practising art therapy in the UK.
www.saa.co.uk – The Society for All Artists is for leisure painters and artists. They have details of professional artists that teach, and they also run online workshops and have a comprehensive materials and accessories shop. The shop offers a discount to members but is also open to non-members.
www.bemindful.co.uk – a website that lists teachers of the eight-week mindfulness course with a search facility to find one in your area. Please note it is important you check teachers' credentials and are satisfied with them before embarking on a course.

Books

Cameron, Julia (1995). *The Artist's Way*. Basingstoke and Oxford: Pan Books.
Gair, Angela (ed.) (1995). *Collins Artist's Manual: The Complete Guide to Painting and Drawing Materials and their Use*. London: HarperCollins.
Greenhalgh, Wendy Ann (2015). *Mindfulness and the Art of Drawing – A Creative Path to Awareness*. Lewes: Leaping Hare Press.
Silverstone, Liesl (2009). 'Art Therapy Exercises – Inspirational and Practical Ideas to Stimulate the Imagination'. London: Jessica Kingsley.
Williams, Mark and Penman, Danny (2011). *Mindfulness: A Practical Guide to Finding Peace in a Frantic World*. London: Piatkus.

Online art shops

www.jacksonsart.com
www.greatart.co.uk
www.hobbycraft.co.uk

Materials are also available from high street stores such as Paperchase, WHSmith, Hobbycraft and Rymans and their online shops.

Index

Page numbers for figures are given in *italics*, and for tables they are given in **bold**. Any reference to figures in the plate section will be given as 'pl'.

abstract images 39, 81
accessories, materials 70, 97
acrylic paint 96
acrylic paper 94
action-orientated clients 45
aha! moment 32–33, 37, 45, 86
ancient art–modern art similarities 8–9
anger 34
archaeology 2–3, 8
art: defining 66; limiting use of 51–52, 55–56; perceptions of 5, 52–54
art shops, materials 97–98
art stories 4, 54, 72
art therapy 12–17; approaches 12, 14–15; benefits 13–14; emergence of 10, 12; potential 3; themes 17
articulate clients 45
artists, perceptions of 52–54
The Artist's Way (Cameron) 102

barriers: to using art 51–55; for coaches 99; overcoming 71–72, *see also* boundaries of work
bias, left-hemisphere 54–55
blockages to writing 49–50
books to read 102
boundaries of work: using art 4; clarifying 66; intent and 62; in practice 89; supervision and 103
brain hemispheres 18–41; art effectiveness 2; bias 54–55; exercises 72; functions 19–37; lateralisation 3, 17, 18; perceptions 11; phonetic languages 9; thinking 79; working with the whole 61
breath, using 79

British Museum, 'Ice-age Art' exhibition 8
brushes 95
business coaching 47–48

Cameron, Julia 102
canvas 93–94
card 93
cartridge paper 93, 105
case study approach 46–51, 90–91
cave paintings 8
censoring images 79
charcoal 95, 106
chicken claw experiment 30–32
clay 96
clear purpose 62; art therapy 16; exercise choice 73
client-centred coaching 59–60
clients: coaches as 102; materials preferences 69; openness 63
clients' art: contracting use of 67; examples *2*; externalising 57, 80–82, *81–82*, 87, pl
closing out programme 90–91
coaches: barriers for 99; being coached 102; building confidence 99–102; current practices 42; developing confidence 102–104; goal-setting 10; lack of confidence 52; managing themselves 87–89; materials preferences 69; principles 62–63; talking/working with others 4–6
coaching/coaching-with-art: current challenges 43–44; explaining approach to 66; framework 65; getting started 99–107; models 12; potential/insights

3; in practice 64–91; preparation for 68–71; principles of 57–63
coaching space *see* space
collage 72, 96–97
colour sticks 96
colouring pencils 94
colours, recurring images 17
comfort zone, stepping out of 56
communication 8–11; archaeology 2–3, 8; psychology 3
comparisons of images 17
complexity: emotional value 33–35; paradox and 44; whole, reconstructing 24–27
confidence: barriers to 52; coaches' 99–104
confidentiality 67
congruence, person-centred approach 60
connecting stage of process 58, 78, 83–86
continuing discoveries 58, 78, 86–87
continuing professional development (CPD) 68
contracting process 15, 65–67, 89
corpus callosum 18, 19, 22, 30–31
counselling models 12
courses for coaches 103–104
CPD *see* continuing professional development
crayons 94–95
creating stage of process 58, 78, 80–82
creativity: confidence-building 99–102; perception barriers 52–54; in play 46; productivity balance 48–49
Csíkszentmihalyi, Mihaly 38, 61
cultural bias 54

deep places: awareness of 66; going to 15–16
demonstrating materials 71
developmental needs, coaches 102–104
direct-in-the-moment approach 32
discoveries: continuing 58, 78, 86–87; meaning and 83–86
Drama Triangle 88–89, *88*
drawing in-the-moment 76
drawing mediums 94–95
duration of sessions 66–67

Edwards, Betty 19, 102
emergence of images, facilitating 78–80
emotional complexity 35, 37
emotional value 33–35
emotions: art therapy 16; tuning in to 45–46
empathetic understanding 59–60
ethics 66, 89
event-based exercises 77

executive coaching 47
exercises: choosing 72–78; introducing 73; types 73–78
experimental practice 91
externalising images 57, 80–82, 87

facilitation process 78–87
felt-tip pens 94
figurative metaphors 28
final session of programme 90–91
first session of programme 71
flow 37–38, 48, 61
found materials 105
frame shifts 29–30, 32
free exercises 76–77, 80
Freud, Sigmund 9

Gazzaniga, Michael 19, 30–31, 33
graphite pencils/sticks 94
group session time management 69
guided exercises: metaphor use 75–76; mindfulness pause 80; scenarios 74–75

Haeyen, Suzanne 14
helping professions 9–10
hemispheres of brain 18–41; art effectiveness 2; bias 54–55; exercises 72; functions 19–37; perceptions 11; phonetic languages 9; thinking 79; working with the whole 61
hemispheric lateralisation 3, 17, 18
Hill, Adrian 10
Hutschemaekers, Giel 14

'Ice-age Art: Arrival of the Modern Mind' (British Museum) 8
image, language of 28, 61–62, 84
imaging stage of process 58, 78–80
in-the-moment drawing 32, 39, 76
Inktense sticks 106
intent and boundaries 62
interview exercise example 74–75
intuition: abstract images 39; left-hemisphere bias 54–55

journal-keeping 101, 103
judgement, play 100
Jung, Carl 10
'just-draw-it' moment 32, 76, 80

Karpman Drama Triangle exercise 88–89, *88*
'keepable' images 46

language: brain hemispheres 36–37; emergence of writing 9; of the image 28, 61–62, 84; using visual language 62
lateralisation of brain 3, 17, 18
LeDoux, Joseph E. 30–31
left-brain interpreter 30, 31, 33
left-handedness 55
left-hemisphere of brain 18–41; bias 54–55; exercises 72; functions 2, **20–21**; phonetic languages 9; quietening 38–39; right-hemisphere interaction 11, **20–21**, 22, 36, 39–40; thinking 79; working with the whole 61
Levy, Jerre 22
lightbulb moment *see* aha! moment
limitations in use of art 51–52, 55–56
line making 85

McGilchrist, Ian 3, 19, 23, 26, 29, 33–34, 54
Malchiodi, Cathy A. 12, 14
The Master and His Emissary (McGilchrist) 3, 19, 23
materials 92–98; choosing 69–70, 80; familiarity with 62; getting started with 104–107; for play 100; portability 55, 70, 105–107; preparation 68–71; process questions 84–85; storing 97
meaning: discovering 83–86; emerging later 16
measurement of coaching programmes 43–44
mediums 92; alternative 96–97; for drawing 94–95; painting/water-based 95–96; for play 100
memorable images 46
memory as barrier 53, 62
metaphor, exercises 75–77
metaphoric thinking 27–29
mindfulness imaging process 74–75
mindfulness pause 38, 79–80
Miracle Question exercise 77
mirroring approach 83, 87–88
modern art–ancient art similarities 8–9

narrative *see* true narrative
Naumburg, Margaret 10
nerve cables *see* corpus callosum
network of support, coaches 104
neuroscience 10–11, 18–19, 22
The New Drawing on the Right Side of the Brain (Edwards) 19, 102
next-generation coaching 5–6, 43

oil paints 96
oil paper 94
oil pastels 95
online art shops 98
organisational clients: brain hemispheres 27; case study 47; expectations 5–6
'otherness' 47

painting mediums 95–96
pans, watercolour paints 95
papers: acrylic/oil 94; cartridge paper 93, 105; pastel paper 93; for play 100; watercolour paper 93
paradoxes 24–26, 44
parts-versus-whole, brain hemisphere differences 24
pastel paper 93
pastels 95
patterns emerging, images 86–87 *see also* themes emerging, images
pencils: colouring 94; graphite 94; water-soluble 96
pens, felt-tip 94
perception barriers 52–54
permissions: photograph-taking 67, 106; sharing images 72
person-centred approach 14–15; managing 87–88; meaning discovery 83; principles of 58–60
personal coaching 48–49, 52
personal confidence, barriers to 52
phonetic languages 9
photographs, permission to take 67, 106
phrase-based imaging exercises 75
physicality of art 34–35, 55, 61, 83, 85
play: brain hemispheres 39; coaches' 100; creative thinking 46; exercises 76–77, 80; first session 71
play dough 96
portability, materials 55, 70, 105–107
portable materials pack 105, 106–107
portfolios 97
practise importance, coaches 103
process questions 84–86
productivity–creativity balance 48–49
professional development 48–49, 68
psychiatry, development of 9
psychology, communication in 3
public spaces 56
purpose 62; art therapy 16; exercise choice 73
puzzle images 24, *25*

question-asking 84–86, 88
quietening left-hemisphere 38–39

recurring images 17
reflective journal-keeping 103
reflective practice, final session 90
reflective space 15
right-hemisphere of brain 18–41; exercises 72; functions 2, **20–21**; left-hemisphere interaction 11, **20–21**, *22*, 36, 39–40; phonetic languages 9; time-free mode 37–38; working with the whole 61
Rogers, Carl 59–60
role model, providing 101
Rubin vase puzzle image 24
rules creation, left hemisphere 29

scenario-based exercises 74–75
second-generation coaching *see* next-generation coaching
self-expression: materials for 92; space for 60
shifts *see* frame shifts; transformational shifts
shodo art 57
silent right-hemisphere, giving a voice 36–37
Silverstone, Leisl 14, 58
slowing the pace 79
social media 9
space: agreeing 66; confidentiality 67; emergence of images 78; experimental practice 91; limitations 56; managing 87; preparation 68; for self-expression 60
speech, left-hemisphere 26, 31, 36
Sperry, Roger W. 19
spiral staircase exercise 24, 25–27, *26*
split-brain studies 19, 30–31
spontaneity 39
stable world creation 29, 30
starter pack, materials 105–106
Stevenson, Liesl 3
sticks: colour sticks 96; graphite 94; Inktense sticks 106
stopping exploration, client 66
storage for materials 97
storytelling brain 31, *see also* art stories

'stuckness' 49–51
'success' 75
Sumerian language 9
supervision 63, 89, 103
support networks, coaches 104
supports, materials 92–94

talking during sessions 80
themes emerging, images 86–87 *see also* patterns emerging, images
therapeutic models 12
thinking, banishing 79
thinking loops 29, 31–32
time-frame of sessions 66–67
time-free mode, right-hemisphere 37–38
time management 69
Tomoko Kawao 57
transformational shifts 5–6, 32–33, 43, 47
true narrative 30–32

unconditional positive regard 60–61
unconscious, tapping into 57
unlocking core issues 5–6, 43, 44, 49–51

van Hooren, Susan 14
visual journal-keeping 101
visual languages: using 62; in written language 9, *see also* language
vocalised speech 36, *see also* speech

Wada test 19
water-based mediums 95–96
water-soluble mediums 96
watercolour paints 95
watercolour paper 93
wax crayons 94–95
whole: brain reconstructing 24–27; working with 24–27, 60–61
word-based imaging exercises 75
words, limitations of 6
workshops for coaches 103–104
writing blockages 49–50
written language, emergence of 9

Yakovlevian torque 22

Colour Image 1 Sam's image of her and the organisation, showing the whole issue and the complexity within it

Colour Image 2 Sam's transformational image of a curl

Colour Image 3 Amelia's desert island; a representation of her new relationship

Colour Image 4 Amelia's aha! moment

Colour Image 5 Keira's breakthrough image 'flow'

Colour Image 6 Keira's breakthrough image 'inner voice'

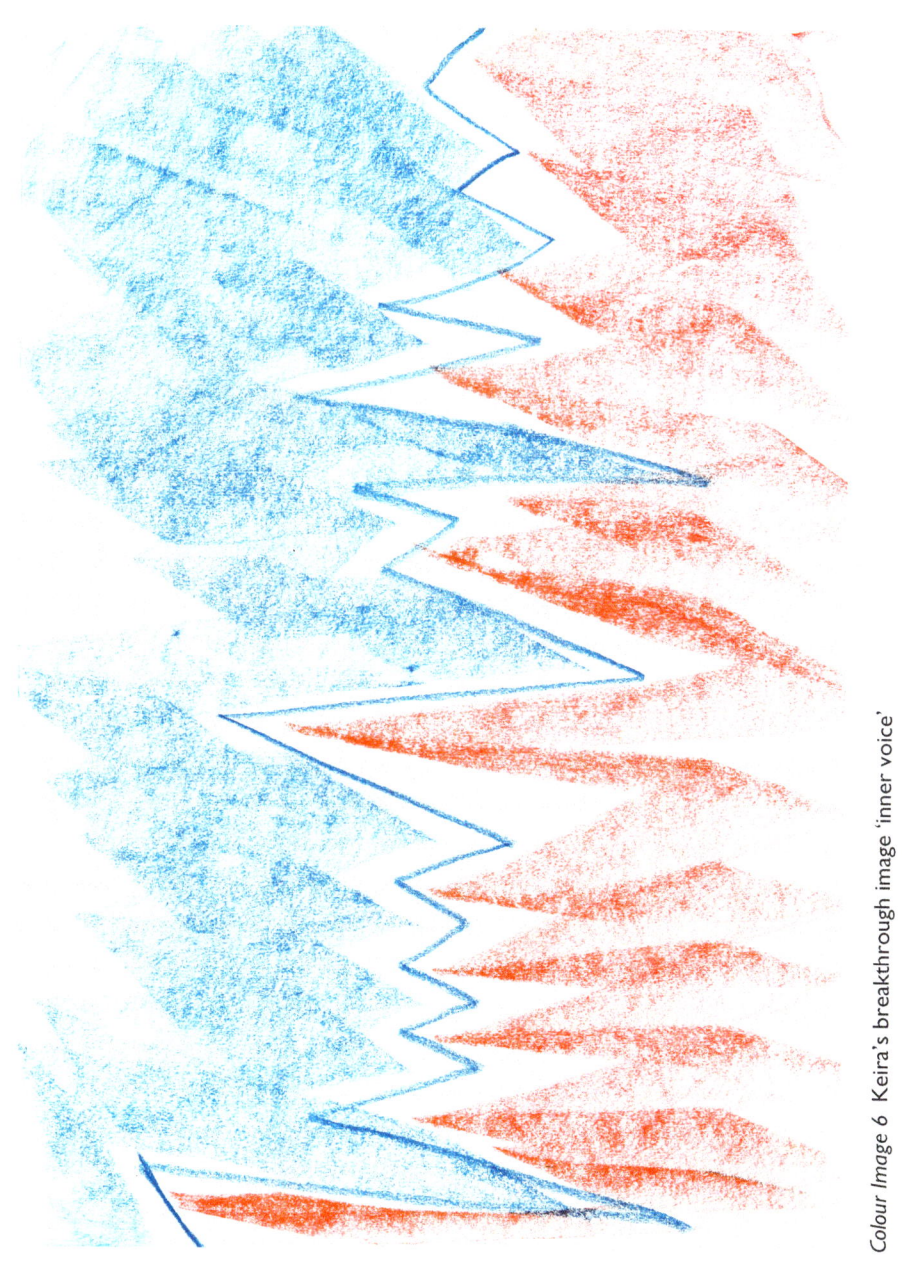

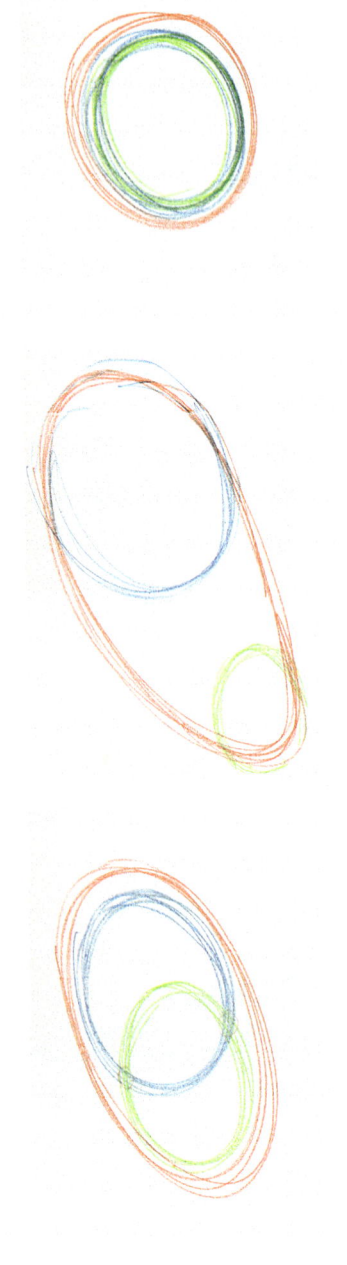

Colour Image 7 James' final images: 'where I was', 'where I am now' and 'where I want to be'

Colour Image 8 Jaye's first image from her first coaching session

Colour Image 9 Jaye's final image, showing her shift out of 'stuckness'

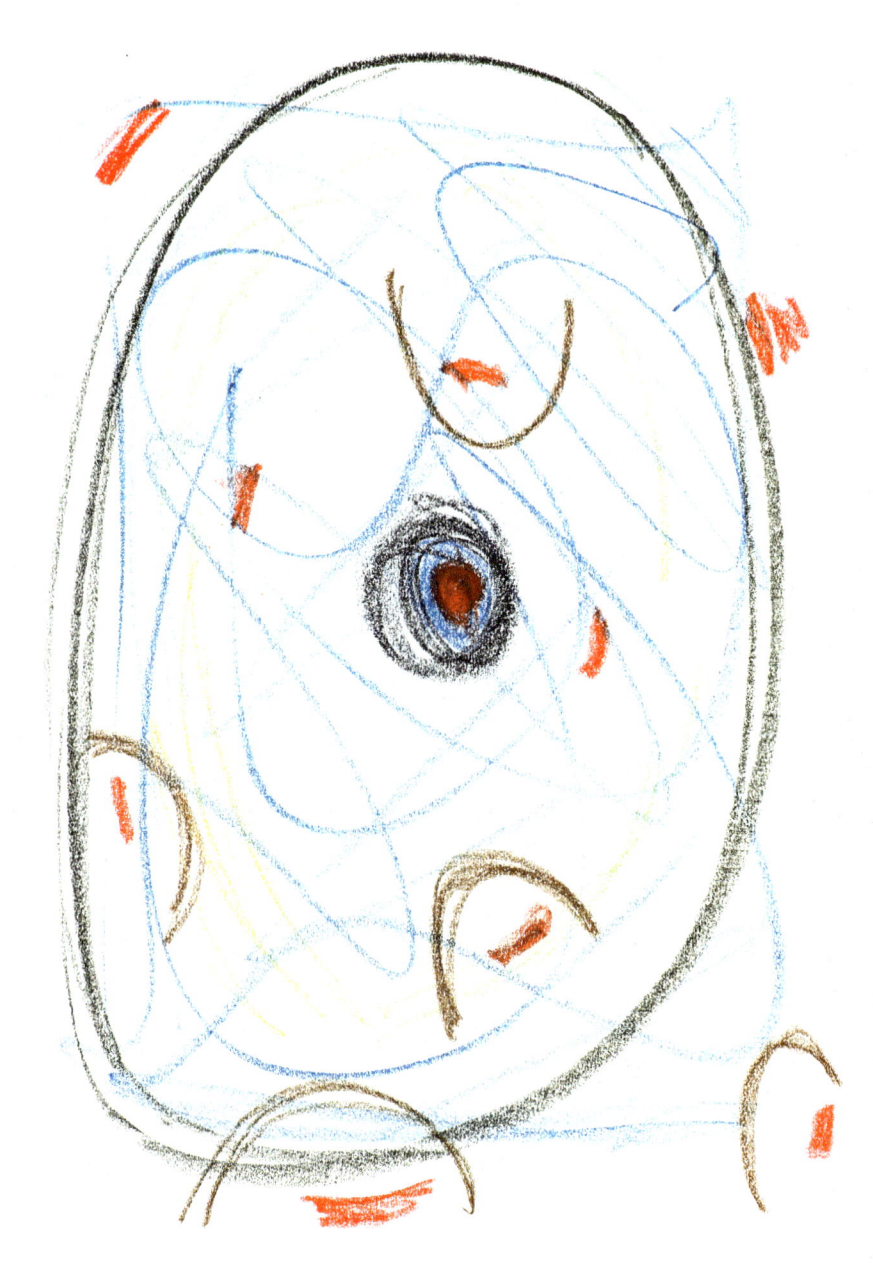

Colour Image 10 James' image from a guided exercise

Colour Image 11 Sam's image from a guided metaphor-based exercise

Colour Image 12 Amelia's initial play image, added to through exploration and coaching in her first session

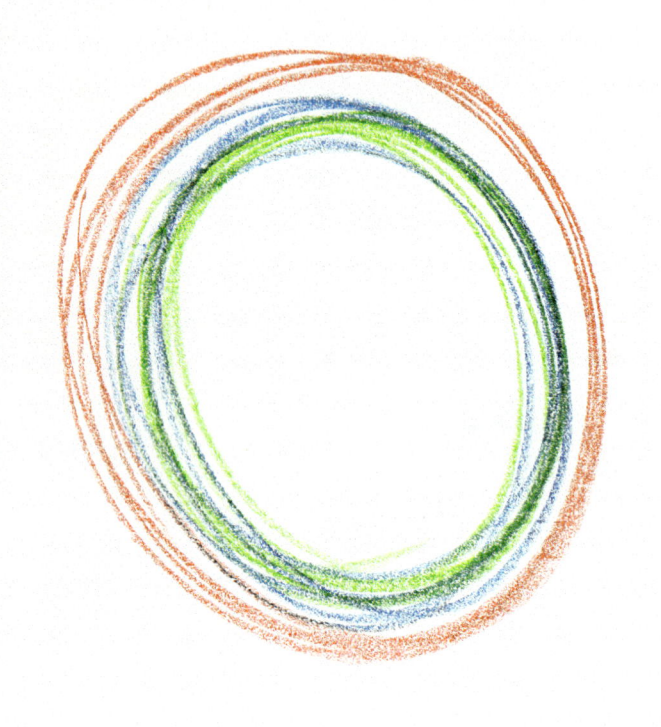

Colour Image 13 James' final image

Colour Image 14 Sam's final image